Hidden in the Rubble

Hidden
in the Rubble

A Haitian Pilgrimage to
Compassion and Resurrection

Photographed and Written by
Gerard Thomas Straub

ORBIS BOOKS
Maryknoll, New York 10545

Founded in 1970, Orbis Books endeavors to publish works that enlighten the mind, nourish the spirit, and challenge the conscience. The publishing arm of the Maryknoll Fathers and Brothers, Orbis seeks to explore the global dimensions of the Christian faith and mission, to invite dialogue with diverse cultures and religious traditions, and to serve the cause of reconciliation and peace. The books published reflect the views of their authors and do not represent the official position of the Maryknoll Society. To learn more about Maryknoll and Orbis Books, please visit our website at www.maryknollsociety.org.

Library of Congress Cataloging-in-Publication Data

Straub, Gerard Thomas, 1947-
  Hidden in the rubble : a Haitian pilgrimage to compassion and resurrection / photographed and written by Gerard Thomas Straub.
    p. cm.
  ISBN 978-1-57075-897-3
1. Poverty—Haiti. 2. Haiti—Social conditions—1971- 3. Haiti—Economic conditions—1971- 4. Haiti—Religion. 5. Haiti Earthquake, Haiti, 2010. 6. Poverty—Haiti—Pictorial works. 7. Haiti—Social conditions—1971—Pictorial works. 8. Haiti—Economic conditions—1971—Pictorial works. 9. Haiti—Religion—Pictorial works. 10. Haiti Earthquake, Haiti, 2010—Pictorial works. I. Title.
  HC153.Z9P677 2010
  972.9407'3—dc22
                    2010014870

This book is lovingly dedicated to
Tony Bellizzi
Mary Catherine Bunting
John Caven
John Dear, SJ
Tom Hinshaw
Karl Holtsnider
Tony Lazzara, MD, SFO
Patti Normile, SFO
Mike Peak
Paul Robie
Kathleen Straub
and
Dee Wallace
Without their unstinting faith in me
my journey with the poor
would not have been possible.

And I want to offer
a special thanks to
to my wonderful sister
Regina Marie Gerhard
whose constant prayers
sustain me.

Without the vision,
friendship and support of
Robert Ellsberg
this book would
not have been possible.

An individual has not started living until he or she can rise above the narrow confines of his or her individualistic concerns to the broader concerns of all humanity.

—MARTIN LUTHER KING, JR.

The whole idea of compassion is based on a keen awareness of the interdependence of all these living beings, which are all part of one another and all involved in one another.

—THOMAS MERTON

I don't know what your destiny will be, but one thing I know—the only ones among you who will be really happy are those who have sought and found how to serve.

—ALBERT SCHWEITZER

The guarantee of one's prayer is not saying a lot of words. The guarantee of one's petition is very easy to know: how do I treat the poor? Because that is where God is.

—ARCHBISHOP OSCAR ROMERO

Contents

Part II. During the Earthquake Emergency

Part III. After the Earthquake

Preface
In the Beginning Was the Film

Some films begin life as a book. This book began life as a film. A film set in Haiti that explored the necessity of compassion. The film hoped to thoroughly documented the life of the poor in one of the most impoverished of nations. The Cité Soleil slum in Port-au-Prince, the capital of Haiti, is the oldest and largest slum in the city. A volunteer on a mission trip with his church said it's "as close to hell as you can get." Half the children in the slum will die before they reach the age of five. At night, some kids are forced to stay up all night and beat the rats away with sticks. In Haiti, corruption and violence abound. The government is dysfunctional and out of money. Garbage is piled up in the streets and alleys. There is virtually no electrical power; people without a generator spend the night in the dark. Hunger and starvation are rampant. People live in unimaginable squalor and eat mud cakes made from clay, dirt, spices, and sugar . . . and contaminated sewage water. And all of these shocking conditions existed before the earthquake.

In such a grim, deadly, and dangerous environment, which existed before the earthquake and which was made monstrously worse after the earthquake, I wanted to offer a visual meditation on compassion, along with a series of reflections on the nature and importance of compassion, which is, of course, a central part of all religions, though you hardly ever see it truly practiced in the daily life of most believers. The footage captured the dignity and courage of the poor, as well as the vibrantly colorful culture of Haiti, along with its music, art, and stunning natural beauty. In the midst of the agony of extreme poverty and deprivation, the footage celebrated the possibility of a better future through mutual cooperation and genuine compassion. Every moment of every day, God the All Powerful willingly becomes powerless and risks literally becoming a beggar of love patiently waiting for us to respond by not only loving God but also all of God's creation, especially the poor and rejected. And compassion is the fullest expression of the luminous force of intentional love and kindness.

The footage vividly captured the dreadful conditions that existed before the earthquake, as well as the massive devastation and loss of life after the earthquake. Without question, the earthquake immediately changed the nature of the film, as well as this book. Part 1 of the book consists primarily of the film's original narration, which described life before the earthquake while also offering reflections on compassion. Part 2 details the immediate aftermath of the earthquake, which I documented while being part of a team of doctors who rushed in to help the countless victims. Part 3 looks at life in the refugee camps nearly three months after the earthquake, where nearly a million people lived without adequate shelter or provisions. Part 3 also contains a series of reflections from people fully engaged in helping the Haitians through their darkest days. These reflections collectively offer a portrait of the monumental scope of the problem of rebuilding the destroyed city while also revealing how their lives were forever altered by being graced with the chance to be at the epicenter of compassion in action and witness the energy of hope in a sea of death. Much of the book plays out against the backdrop of Advent (2009) and Lent (2010); insights from those two liturgical seasons offer us a way to enter into the suffering of the poor and to consider how to respond to their pressing needs. In a sense, the book is a journey from Christmas to Easter, from the Incarnation to the Resurrection. It is my prayer that *Hidden in the Rubble* helps you embrace the absolute necessity of true compassion.

Prelude
The Earthquake

On January 12, 2010, I gave a ninety-minute presentation titled "Poverty and Prayer" to an all-girls Catholic high school just outside of Los Angeles. It was a brilliantly sunny, beautiful Tuesday morning. My presentation was a mixture of clips from my many documentary films on global and domestic poverty and personal reflections on my journey from atheism to Christianity, from a network television producer to an advocate for the poor. After showing painful footage of naked, starving kids in Uganda, I spoke extemporaneously from my heart about Haiti. As I spoke, I became very emotional . . . and on the verge of tears. It had been almost four weeks since I had returned home from a week of filming in Port-au-Prince, and I was still haunted by what I had seen, haunted by the distressing sight of little girls and women squatting in rotting garbage to urinate and defecate. The five hundred girls sat in stunned silence as they watched, through tears in their eyes, the dire conditions kids their age endure in far-away places well beyond the scope of their awareness or interest. As I drove back to my studio, I pondered the stark contrast between the privileged lives of the girls at this private high school and the disadvantaged lives of the kids in Cité Soleil. Then, a scant few hours later, a friend from ABC News called to say that moments ago a powerful earthquake had struck Haiti.

As the hours rolled on, the scope of the tragedy intensified. The initial news reports and images were horrifying. By Wednesday, the world was beginning to understand the extent of the massive damage and the horrific loss of life. Port-au-Prince had been leveled, completely destroyed . . . and perhaps 100,000 people were crushed in poorly constructed, collapsed buildings. Everyone said it was a huge disaster; but in reality, Haiti was an immense disaster before the 7.0 earthquake. Prior to that tragic Tuesday, the margin of life in Haiti was already narrow; after the earthquake, it was razor thin. Before the earthquake, Haiti had a vast reservoir of airborne illnesses; after, the tens of thousands of decaying corpses deepened it into an abyss.

Three full days after the earthquake, little help had reached the desperate people of Port-au-Prince, many of whom had gone without water and food since their world literally tumbled down around them. The immense international aid effort was slowed to a crawl, handicapped by debris-strewn roads, a badly damaged port, and a single-runway airport that was unable to handle the influx of large cargo planes. Planes with vitally important aid were delayed in landing, forced to circle for hours, or worse, diverted to the Dominican Republic.

The chaos and congestion at the airport revealed just how inept, crippled, and unreliable the Haitian government was. Port-au-Prince was an endless refugee camp, with an estimated 300,000 people sleeping in the open, raising the threat of cholera and other infectious diseases to even more dangerous levels than before. One hospital had collapsed, and eight of the remaining thirteen hospitals were seriously damaged. People with life-threatening head injuries or crushed limbs requiring immediate surgery were left untreated. Without antibiotics or medications, serious infections were left to fester. Underequipped mobile operating theaters in hastily pitched tents performed emergency amputations, sometimes with rusty hacksaws. Some surgeries were performed outdoors at night with illumination provided by a single flashlight. There was not even enough alcohol to sterilize the instruments. An American doctor who was there during the first week after the earthquake called it a "mass casualty horror show." Hospitals outside of Port-au-Prince were performing life-saving surgeries around the clock; but they were no match for the overwhelming need. It was estimated that 250,000 people were injured during the earthquake, and 1.5 million people where left homeless. Many of the homeless headed for the countryside to escape the bedlam of the ruined city.

Day by day, the resentment and anger within the frightened sur-

vivors began to boil over into sporadic pockets of looting and violence. Gunfire added to the hyper-charged chaos. Three days after
the earthquake only about 9,000 of the dead had been buried, most
in mass graves, and at least ten times that number were lying uncovered and unidentified on the streets or under mounds of rubble. The
air was toxic with the nauseating stench of decaying bodies. The psychological impact of seeing so many corpses further traumatized the
survivors, especially the children. After one week, 70,000 bodies had
been recovered, and the death toll was estimated to be a jaw-dropping 200,000. Bulldozers scooped up the dead, dropped them into a
dump truck, which was driven to the site of a mass grave, and buried
them without mourning, without prayers, without dignity. The dead
were simply a health hazard that had to be removed. And as the people lost confidence in the government's ability to remove the corpses,
they took matters in their own hands and burned them right were
they lay. Hopelessness, desperation, grief, and death lingered in the
air . . . just as it had, to a lesser extent, before the earthquake.

Nine days after the earthquake, I landed in Port-au-Prince with
twenty-two doctors and nurses from all across the States in a chartered 737 jet jammed with medical supplies. And during the week I
was in Haiti, I saw devastation so severe and so widespread that
words fail to capture the magnitude of it, both in terms of the damage to buildings and the injuries to people. One doctor said he had
never seen so many people with multiple serious injuries. In the
midst of the rubble of a mountainside shanty town in which virtually all the homes were destroyed, a survivor looked at me and said,
"Everything is dead."

The earthquake rattled my plans for the film. Things I had captured on camera were no longer there. I had to resist the temptation
to refocus the film on the current news-making disaster. From its
inception, the film was about compassion, and I could not let it
become solely about the earthquake. Long before that dreadful
Tuesday, compassion was hidden in the shadows of Haitian life, hidden by the innate force of survival, and the common good took a
backseat to a cold, cutthroat individualism where everyone looks out
only for himself or herself. The all pervasive individualism and lack
of any sense of solidarity does not stem from a spirit of selfishness but

is born from the primal instinct for personal survival and from, as Tom Roberts of the *National Catholic Reporter* notes, a "residue from the brutal era of the dictatorship of the Duvalier family, a period during which any hint of political organizing could mean death." I filmed inside the abandoned prison "Papa Doc" Duvalier built, where perhaps as many as 60,000 Haitians were killed. You could almost hear the shrieking screams of torture and agony. The prison is a monument to how corrupt, unstable, and violent politics can be in Haiti. Recently, a senator was assassinated, and his twenty-three-year-old assistant, who was loyal to deposed President Jean-Bertrand Aristide, was burned alive. Today, the empty concrete cells of the prison are used as toilets by some of the residents of Cité Soleil. The irony is not missed in this act of defiant necessity.

The earthquake was actually almost irrelevant to the real story. The real story was that Haiti was already a mind-boggling disaster long before the earthquake, but, outside of a few dedicated relief agencies and individuals, no one noticed, no one cared. And within weeks of the wall-to-wall, breathless coverage of the immediate aftermath of the earthquake, which detailed the gruesome carnage and the horrific images of countless corpses strewn about the streets like litter, the news crews went home and moved onto another story, another headline. But the poor of Haiti were still there, still homeless, still hungry, still hurting from their injuries, still suffering from the great loss of life. Due to the news coverage, millions upon millions of dollars flowed into Haiti. But questions lingered: Where did that money go? How was it used? Did corruption raise its ugly head again, stealing aid and lining the pockets of the powerful? In truth, I wasn't so interested in finding the answers to those very legitimate questions. I feared I already knew the answer . . . and didn't like it. My interest, in both the film and this book, was much simpler, much more basic: compassion . . . and its deeper, ongoing meaning for our lives, our survival.

Let's pause for a moment and take a brief look at life in Haiti before the earthquake. An astounding lack of compassion has marked Haiti's history. In a very real way, Haiti's past is a prologue to the earthquake. A seasoned relief worker who was familiar with dire poverty around the world arrived in Haiti shortly before I began filming in December of 2009 and said he had "not seen anything like

this before." Eighty percent of the ten million Haitians lived in poverty, 54 percent in abject poverty. Most of the poor were lucky to earn two bucks in a day. The unemployment rate before the earthquake stood at 60 percent, and the exodus of skilled workers such as doctors, lawyers, and architects to the United States and beyond crippled the economy even more. One percent of Haiti's population owns half of the nation's wealth. Haiti is a corridor for hurricanes and tropical storms. In a three-week period in 2008, three hurricanes and one tropical storm had struck Haiti. Many people lost all their crops and livestock to the storms, compounding the daily struggle to feed their families. The combination of steep and deforested hillsides with flood-prone areas makes the country particularly vulnerable to the onslaught of destructive weather patterns. Roads and bridges were washed away, making some places impossible to reach.

More than a year after this particular series of natural disasters, the people of Haiti were still struggling to recover. The rising food prices led to civil unrest. Before the earthquake, a third of the population still did not have a guaranteed supply of food. They woke up hungry every day; and every day, a search for food was their top priority. Chronic malnutrition affected 24 percent of the children, and that rose to as high as 40 percent in the poorest parts of Haiti. Local food production only covered 42 percent of the population's needs. Haiti is one of the most ecologically devastated countries on earth. Most of the trees have been cut down and turned into cooking charcoal. Through poverty and ignorance, hillsides were denuded, creating rampant soil erosion. And that dark picture gets even bleaker when considering some less visibly tangible realities. More than 50 percent of the women in Haiti are illiterate. Most rural Haitians do not understand how people get AIDS or other serious diseases. And perhaps most distressing, because people in poverty often lack awareness of basic human rights, they are easily manipulated into "selling" their children into various forms of servitude to pay off a debt to a moneylender.

One night after filming, I sat alone in my hotel room thinking about the appalling misery I had witnessed that day. I wrote the following in my journal:

> *Despite the magnificent natural beauty of Haiti, Haiti is an ugly place because wide-scale suffering is accepted and allowed to flourish. People are quick to offer an array of historical, social, and political reasons for the poverty, but no one really wants to end it or at least there is no collective will to end it. The government is corrupt. The infrastructure is woefully inadequate for the growing population. Haiti is a dismal place, teeming with anger and rage and broken, empty promises.*
>
> *From my perspective, at least on a purely rational level, the sit-*

uation in Haiti is virtually hopeless. No amount of well-intentioned "projects" is going to make a difference. For things to change, the hearts of people in Haiti and around the world must be broken. We are all to blame for Haiti.

The only hope I see resides in an understanding of Christ and the demands of the gospel. And that understanding begins with entering more fully into the mystery of the humility of God.

And that is what I hope to do in this book.

The earthquake has broken the hearts of the people of Haiti, and the hearts of people all around the world. In that darkest of moments, we were given a chance to look more deeply at our own lives, to see more clearly our own self-centeredness, our own inability to share our lives and resources. We were given a chance to truly see the self-emptying love that Christ asks from his followers. The earthquake showed us the fragility of life and the power of nature. But a good percentage of the stupendous loss of life was not the fault of trembling nature. Many deaths were unnecessary and were caused by human failure. It was callous and greedy humans who did not care enough to build safer structures for the chronically poor or have emergency relief plans ready to help those living in such a disaster-prone area. The earthquake gave us a chance to see the importance of putting the common good before individual concerns.

Just as an old cloak cannot take a new patch or old wineskins new wine, the tired old responses to the plight of the poor in Haiti will not work in the face of the complete devastation of Haiti. Recovery will require new solutions, new heights of human ingenuity, and new levels of compassion. Just stumbling forward is not an option for the well-being of millions of Haitians. They need us . . . and we need them.

Filtered through the cruel reality of the intense, widespread, dire poverty of Haiti, *Hidden in the Rubble* is about the true beauty and transformative power of compassion. The earthquake has given all of us a chance to enter more fully into the beauty and necessity of compassion. I think of this book as a pilgrimage to a deeper understanding of compassion, a pilgrimage into the broken heart of Haiti. And the pilgrimage, for me, began two months before the earthquake.

Part 1

Before the Earthquake

Prologue: Glimpses of Hope

It was a sunny Sunday in the middle of November 2009. A friend had invited me to attend a worship service at an Episcopal church in Pasadena. Much to my surprise, the homily touched me, as it poignantly addressed the necessity of compassion. The subject of the rector's powerful sermon was simple, yet the implications were enormous. He wanted the congregation to pledge allegiance to compassion and to the human family for which it stands. The inspiring homily resonated within me for days.

Weeks later, on December 9 (during the second week of Advent), that homily unexpectedly led me to Port-au-Prince and deeper into the heart of compassion. Compassion is the fullest expression of the luminous force of intentional love and kindness. Humanity's survival hinges on that one word . . . compassion is our sole hope. Compassion is at the heart of all religious and spiritual traditions. When we enter the heart of compassion, we enter the heart of God.

I've been making documentary films on poverty around the world since 1998. When I look into the sad face of a starving child living on the margins of a horrific slum, I find myself looking into the very mystery of life, a mystery so profound that it can't even be spoken. Chronic poverty, with its desperate and endless struggle for survival, fills me with grief. Yet these dreadful and hopeless slums became for me sacraments of transcendence that helped me awake from my self-centered slumber and led me to a place of more authentic solidarity with the poor. In these dreadful places of extreme desperation I often caught glimpses of hope and the quivering feeling that life is truly magnificent and precious. Here I learned to see that some things can't be reduced to the cognitive. The cross is clearly visible in these nightmarish slums, but so is the joy of the Resurrection, and the understanding that there is meaning that goes on beyond us. Here God is hidden in the suffering, hidden in the rubble of our lives, hidden in great and small acts of resurrection, hidden in a truly inexhaustible mystery.

But there is no mystery about this: the world is riddled with pain. No life can escape it. Even Jesus experienced it. Pain is universal. When we turn our attention away from our own pain, we can see the pain of others, the pain of the world.

Once we truly see and feel the suffering of others, we are impelled to alleviate it. In the process we slowly come to realize we are not the center of the universe and that all living creatures possess an inviolable sanctity that binds us together as sisters and brothers.

Over and over again, Christ tells us that love is the sole criterion for eternal unity with God. This love is far from a mere humanitarian concern for abstract justice and the anonymous "poor."

Christ calls us to a concrete and personal love for all people, including our enemies, and for all of creation. He calls us to be his helping, healing hands. Christ someday will say to us, "When I was hungry, you gave me something to eat." When we soothe the trials of others, we encounter Christ. We are called to be angels of compassion, God's messengers delivering food and hope to those living with hunger and despair.

Advent reminds us that God humbly and continuously bends down in love to embrace us in our weakness and vulnerability. God's love is different from our love. God's love means being willing to love someone more than your own life, for the sake of the other. Every moment of every day, God is begging for our love and seeking out compassionate souls to express this love, especially to the poor and rejected.

Advent

As my friends and neighbors were busy shopping for Christmas presents, I was landing in a place where the joy of Christmas is about as far removed from the everyday reality of the lives of the poor as is the tiny town of Bethlehem from my home in Burbank, California.

In one of the readings of the Second Sunday of Advent, the prophet Isaiah says the Lord sent him "to bring glad tidings to the lowly, to heal the brokenhearted, to proclaim liberty to the captives." This too is our task. In Haiti, it was easy to see how Christmas is a time for us to emulate, as best we can, God's love and goodness by sharing the mercy and compassion we have experienced through our lived experience of Christ's birth in the stable of our humble hearts.

In the slums of Haiti, I am stripped bare of all pretensions, all sense of superiority. I am stripped bare of all that I love and all that is familiar. And I stand in the midst of the swirling, turbulent world of overwhelming want, feeling the pain and not knowing how to respond. But God says, "Let my eyes, my hands, my mouth become your eyes, your hands, your mouth. With my eyes, see their dignity and beauty; with my hands, give a warm embrace, and with my mouth, say a kind word and offer a smile to each sad face. To the person who has become hardened and hopeless, give them my heart."

This is the gift of Christmas: the heart of God born afresh within each of us.

City of the Sun

The name sounds enchanting . . . Cité Soleil. The name means "City of the Sun." But even under the stunningly bright Caribbean sun, Cité Soleil is a dark and dangerous place, a slum so wretched few outsiders enter it. More than a quarter million people are crammed in the three dense square miles that make up Cité Soleil, the largest and oldest slum in the sprawling capital city of Port-au-Prince.

They live in rusting peak-roofed tin shacks. Open sewers and the stench of rotting garbage intensify the brutally ugly reality. Kids run around naked or in tattered clothes, and many of them have never been to school. With the rat population outnumbering people ten to one, the nights bring on even more horrors. Children must find sticks and beat away the diseased rodents throughout the night, to keep from being bit as they try to sleep.

People are so hungry they eat "cakes" made of clay, dirt, spices, sugar . . . and filthy, contaminated water. Pigs rummage alongside kids in search of food buried in the dense rubbish. People are sometimes forced to give up their kids to servitude because they can't afford to feed them. There is virtually no electrical power. Nights are spent in nearly total darkness. When it rains at night, the rain seeps into the shacks and the poor sleep in the mud. Fetid canals thick with noxious garbage run through Cité Soleil.

Women and children squat in the rancid, insect-infested rubbish to defecate and urinate without the dignity of privacy. Many children have worms, which eat up to 20 percent of a child's nutritional intake every day. Haitians are among the poorest-fed children in the world, and no child there can afford to lose 20 percent of his or her food. The effects of such losses are anemia, vitamin deficiencies, a weakened immune system, lethargy, and poor cognitive development. Intestinal worms magnify the impact of chronic diarrhea from bad water, common in all parts of Port-au-Prince. Half the newborn children in Cité Soleil will die before they reach the age of five.

And if all of that is not bad enough, Cité Soleil is riddled with unbridled violence. There is little police presence, and reformers are routinely assassinated. Guns and gangs rule the slums. People are decapitated or burned alive for opposing the neighborhood gang leader. Murder, rape, kidnapping, looting, and shootings are common, as every area of a few blocks is controlled by one of more than thirty armed factions. Lawlessness was so pervasive it wasn't even uncommon for UN peacekeepers to be killed in Cité Soleil. Few residents live past the age of fifty; they die from disease, including AIDS, or violence. Death is in the air.

The neighborhood, originally designed to house manual laborers for a local export processing zone known as EPZ, quickly became home to squatters from around the countryside looking for work in the newly constructed factories. After a 1991 coup d'état deposed President Jean-Bertrand Aristide, a boycott of Haitian products closed the EPZ. Cité Soleil was soon thrust into extreme poverty and persistent unemployment, with high rates of illiteracy.

The residents of Cité Soleil live in the shadows. There are no stores, no job opportunities, no social services. They live virtually in exile and at the mercy of gangs, local politicians, and global economic forces beyond their control. The grinding poverty and desperate daily search for food have left them literally numb to the normal aspects of life. Yet in the darkness, there are gentle rays of light. Every day in Cité Soleil, grace and violence, blessing and bloodshed intermingle, as the joy of the crib of Christ and the pain of the cross of Christ are both present.

It's a Small World

Nearly twenty years ago, a man walked into this lawless nightmare under the sun, a gentle, humble, funny man from Philadelphia. A former chaplain at Princeton University, he seemed ill-suited by temperament and training to be a beacon of hope in such a hopeless place. His name is Father Tom Hagan. He is a member of the Oblates of Saint Francis de Sales. Father Tom is the embodiment of the luminous force of intentional kindness and compassion.

The hallmark of Saint Francis de Sales's spirituality is gentleness. The saint stressed the importance of the *via media*, the middle way that maintains a true center between all extremes . . . except for the love of God in which alone can we afford to be extreme. Saint Francis de Sales is the patron saint of journalists because of the many tracts and books he wrote. In his most famous book, *Introduction to the Devout Life*, written in 1608, he wrote: "To make divine love live and reign in us, we must kill self-love, and if we cannot entirely annihilate it at least we weaken it in such a way that though it lives yet it does not reign over us."

Father Tom has truly followed that wise advice. He lives, not for himself, but for the forgotten and anguished people of Cité Soleil. And he does so at great risk to his own life. Father Tom, with his dog, Julia, at his side, is a sign of Christ's love as he humbly confronts the countless trials and tribulations of slum life and, through his wonderful nonprofit organization Hands Together, tries to comfort, encourage, educate, feed, and care for the victims of oppression living in the shadow of death known as Cité Soleil.

How I met Father Tom is one of those surprisingly delicious stories that illustrates the old Disney theme song, "It's a small world after all." Back in the late 1990s while I was writing my book on Saint Francis of Assisi, *The Sun and Moon Over Assisi,* I was struggling to understand the saint's love not only for the poor but for poverty itself. It made no sense to me. I had lived such a pampered life that I didn't even know any poor people. Saint Francis may have chased after Lady Poverty, but I chased after Brother BMW.

For Saint Francis, voluntary poverty was a way for him to always be dependent on God for everything. I could perhaps understand that on a theoretical level, but on a practical level, it was very difficult to grasp, especially in our culture that promotes personal strength and independence. In order to better understand, I lived for a month with Franciscan friars serving at St. Francis Inn, a humble little soup kitchen that truly acknowledges the dignity of each person who enters it. The inn was located in the Kensington section of Philadelphia, which was one of the worst slums in America. Known as The Badlands, Kensington was a dangerous and foreboding place where drugs and violence were as common as a cold. The residents were truly marginalized and forgotten; they lived in fear and in overwhelming want. The first night I was there, a little girl was killed by a stray bullet. It was winter, and a number of people sleeping in abandoned buildings froze to death. Rats were more common than cats. I wanted to leave almost as soon as I got there. Yet in that dreadful place my life was transformed.

Every conception I had about the homeless and the addicted turned out to be a misconception. I met real people, people just like me in so many ways. It's easy to label a homeless person as lazy or an alcoholic or drug addict as weak. The labels removed my obligation to do anything . . . it's their fault they are homeless, it's their fault they are addicted. Christ didn't label people or judge people . . . he reached out to them, he excluded no one.

The people whom I once blithely dismissed as worthless and those who were dedicating their lives to serving them moved me to want to make a film about the St. Francis Inn, and that decision lead to the founding of the San Damiano Foundation.

Before going to Haiti, a friend of mine who attends Holy Family Catholic Church in South Pasadena told me about Father Tom. His parish supports Father Tom's ministry to the poor of Cité Soleil. I called Father Tom's number in Haiti many times before leaving but had no luck connecting with him. I did send him an e-mail and gave him my cell phone number, which would work in Haiti. The first night in Haiti, Father Tom called. I was stunned to hear him say he had read my book *The Sun and Moon Over Assisi* and had actually seen the second film I made on the St. Francis Inn, *Room at the Inn*. Implausible as this seemed, Father Tom explained that he had actually worked as a regular volunteer at the St. Francis Inn in its early days. We knew many of the same people. The next morning I drove to his home . . . and I was greeted like a long-lost old friend. We energetically talked nonstop about Philly, Haiti, poverty, faith, and God for more than an hour. It was delightful. Then he escorted me through the slums of Cité Soleil for the first of two extensive walking tours of the area.

It was clear that the people really loved and respected him. Everywhere we went he was surrounded by people. But in one particular section of Cité Soleil, Father Tom turned to me and said, "In this neighborhood just because you are with me doesn't make it safe. Someone put a gun to my head here just a few weeks ago." I said, "Are you going in?" He answered, "I have to go in, but you have a choice." I said, "Well, I choose to go with you."

Genuine Presence

Why would I choose to go into a dreadful slum such as Cité Soleil? In slums around the world I've encountered genuine holiness in the person of people like Father Tom, people who live out of some truly deeper level of kindness than most of us ever reach. And in these slums I see the wounded body of Christ crying out for help. In these slums I see the light and dark sides of myself. In these slums I gain a clearer sense of perspective . . . about myself and life. In these slums I see how defenseless and vulnerable we all are, how precarious the

human situation is. Every day people die from the icy cold of indifference and loneliness.

In Cité Soleil the beauty of human warmth and genuine presence,
as embodied by a servant of God such as Father Tom, are put in sharp-
er contrast to the impersonal values of profit and efficiency that dom-
inate the world beyond the slums. Contemporary society, with its
ever-accelerating pace of life, is becoming increasingly fragmented
and superficial. We're in such a hurry we don't take time for simple
acts of kindness. Kindness may be the Dalai Lama's religion, but, sadly,
most people worship on the altar of self-interest. I know I did for most
of my life. To spend time in massive slums around the world, or even
in a soup kitchen in your own city, is an effective way to shed our ten-
dency toward self-interest and to more eagerly reach out to those who
are hungry and hurting because of chronic, unjust poverty.

In Cité Soleil, you can graphically see the impact the disastrous
escalation in basic commodity prices has on the poor who do not

have regular access to sufficient amounts of food and water, and who face hunger on a daily basis. Part of the reason for the rising cost of wheat, corn, rice, and soybeans can be traced to commodity market speculation traders fleeing the collapsing derivatives market into safer bets in foodstuffs. Food should not be treated as just another commodity, as every human has the right to enough food to sustain life. Today, more than one billion people are undernourished, and one child dies every six seconds because of malnutrition. In the light of such an overwhelming (and underreported) disaster, compassion compels us to put the common good ahead of greed and profits.

Extending compassion to all people, even our enemies, is the very heart of the Christian faith. You can't receive what you don't give. Jesus said, "Give and it will be given to you. Good measure, pressed down, shaken together, running over, will be put in your lap." In other words, in the jargon of today, outflow determines inflow. Jesus makes it abundantly clear that compassion is to be our central spiritual practice. And through compassion, we are better able to control greed and work together for the equitable distribution of the resources of God's creation through the fullest utilization of humanity's creative ingenuity, so that one day soon there will be no hunger on planet Earth.

Even during these stressful and uncertain economic times, the year ends in a flurry of shopping all across America. Advent helps us see the need to pause and contemplate the deep and magnificent meaning of the Incarnation: that God, in a supreme act of Self-emptying love, became poor for us, entering fully into our flawed humanity in order that we could have the chance to enter more fully into God's perfect divinity. The primary motivation for God's Incarnation is God's goodness, not human sinfulness. The Incarnation is a dynamic expression of God's overflowing love and mercy, as well as a revelation of God's poverty and humility. Christmas is a time for us to see more clearly our own poverty and weakness in order to better receive the gift of God's transforming love. Being in Haiti during Advent helped me better see how we are called to live in the expectancy of a changed world, a world of universal sufficiency and no hunger, a world of peace and nonviolence, a world where the reign of God is fully manifested.

Three Things

Scripture makes it abundantly clear that God asks three things of us: To walk humbly with God, to love kindness, and to do justice.

To love kindness is more than just being nice. It means to enter into relationships of solidarity with the entire human community by being patient with and attentive to all whom we encounter.

And to do justice is more than being fair. It means we cannot tolerate injustice, and must intervene when the powerful abuse the powerless; it requires us to change systems of institutionalized injustice that imprison people in chains of poverty and hunger. We need to be willing to lay down our own lives for the sake of those whose lives have been stolen from them.

Institutionalized injustice can be found everywhere, in every nation. Cité Soleil in Port-au-Prince is no different from Skid Row in Los Angeles. Both are disgraceful abominations in the eyes of God, and God demands we dismantle those prisons and set the captives free. Sadly, we avert our eyes and pretend Cité Soleil and Skid Row are not there. But they are there, and people are suffering.

May God have mercy on them . . . and on us.

Morning Prayer

Father Tom rises every morning at 4:15 a.m., and heads straight for the kitchen to make some coffee in a small percolator. As soon as the coffee is ready, he takes the percolator and a cup to the little chapel on the second floor in order to spend time alone. The chapel is small and simple. The walls are decorated with folk-art type paintings of saints who loved the poor and people who had been murdered in Cité Soleil while serving the poor with Father Tom. Father Tom says that this is the most important part of his day, and he jealously guards this early morning time of stillness and silence. Living in a home with about twenty seminarians and about that many homeless street kids is not easy, and so he has become very protective of this sliver of time and space which he needs to nurture himself. He places the coffee pot and cup on a small table next to his large, wicker rocking chair. A candle burns next to the coffee. He reads his

Jerusalem Bible by the light of a flame in a lantern, as electricity is an occasional visitor, dropping in and out without notice. He reads a passage and then meditates on the words.

He speaks to the Lord. He often says to God, "Lord, why am I here?" He told me there are days when he can't stand Haiti. Actually, a lot of days. He admitted that working with the poor is hard. "They are always pulling at me, always needing something. Some days it's hard to get out, because so many are waiting outside the gate to ask me for something." He candidly told me that he could not survive without his early morning prayer time. Alone in the privacy of the humble chapel, he looks to God and honestly expresses his anger and shares his fears. He said, "Some days I tell God I can't get through another day." At night, he returns to the chapel before going to bed . . . and thanks God for getting him through another day, despite his failures and shortcomings.

The stillness of the chapel helps Father Tom go through the desert of his doubts. Despite his truly heroic work, he comes across as someone truly perplexed by his role. In his chapel he told me he has genuine conversations with God. In his chapel Father Tom, it seems to me, grapples with God. He said some missionaries love Haiti. "I don't get that," he said, adding, "Loving Haiti is a special gift, which I have not received." His gift, he said, is his growing awareness on his dependence upon God. Being in Haiti has taken him deeper into prayer and deepened his experience of God.

He says Mass every morning at 6:30 a.m. in the nearby convent of the sisters of Mother Teresa. He said, "It like having a strong cup of coffee," which helps him get through the day and keeps him from falling apart.

In his book *Hidden Holiness*, Michael Plekon, an Orthodox priest, writes: "Feeling close to God, even believing to hear his voice with a mission, does not spare one from the loss of such strong communion. It does not immunize a person to doubt, discouragement, perhaps even failure." Being with Father Tom helped me see more clearly that it is possible to love, even without any hint of inner confidence and consolation.

In my book *Thoughts of a Blind Beggar*, I described a moment of profound grace in an empty church in Rome in 1995 which forever

changed my life, a fleeting moment when God broke through the silence and allowed me to float on a sea of immense love. Nothing like that moment has ever happened again, and for the most part I walk alone along a path of dry, parched, waterless land nourished only by an occasional cup of cool water from strangers like Father Tom whose fractured humanity does not hinder his fidelity to God.

Solidarity with the Vulnerable

In the busyness of preparing for Christmas it is easy not to see the hungry and homeless hovering in the shadows. Our attitude toward the poor is linked to our attitude toward God. Sadly, our inept response to God's saving love for us is reflected in our failure to love the poor and to serve and care for them without question and as our neighbors. The love of God and the love of neighbor cannot be separated; they are so mutually intertwined as to be one and the same thing.

Jesus is not looking for us to give the poor our spare change; he is asking us to give our very lives. The radical message of Jesus clearly indicates that consuming more than we need is actually stealing from those in need, which is certainly a message our consumer-crazed society does not want to hear.

Jesus never treated people as beggars. Instead he entered into solidarity with the vulnerable, as he did with the man born blind. Jesus shows us that charity is not just about giving, but requires that the giver and receiver become engaged in a human partnership of shared dignity, part of a continuing process of creation, a striving toward a completeness that ensures bringing everyone together and caring about mutual dignity and respect for all.

What Should We Do?

The gospel reading for the Third Sunday of Advent contained a question and an answer: "The crowds asked John the Baptist, 'What should we do?' He said to them in reply, 'Whoever has two cloaks should share with the person who has none. And whoever has food should do likewise.'"

John spoke in spirit and power, saying simply and clearly what we must do. What if you lived in Cité Soleil? How would you like people to treat you? This is how we should treat those who do live there. Water for the thirsty, bread for the hungry, a strong hand for the uncertain: these are what Jesus promises and asks us to deliver.

Through the prophet Isaiah, God says: "Turn to me and be safe, all you ends of the earth, for I am God; there is no other!" Knowingly or unknowingly, the world hungers for the redeeming presence of Christ. The poor and the powerless who seek the Lord in poverty of heart shall be fed the food that truly satisfies.

Cité Soleil is a great place to prepare your heart for the coming of Jesus, in whose Incarnation humanity and divinity are joined in communion. God is coming, of this there is no doubt; the only question is, will we be ready to receive God? And that is a very big question, one which I really don't like facing because it will mean change in the way I live.

A Time to Listen

Being in Haiti during Advent focused my attention on the Incarnation more fully than normal. My thoughts drifted to Mary. Like the poor of Haiti, she too was virtually a nonperson, an outsider living on the margins of her society, a lower-class working girl, effectively invisible and forgotten, when God unexpectedly broke through history and touched her in a special way, bestowing upon her an unimagined dignity.

It seems that God chooses to bring about change by working through people and the routine circumstances of their lives. Mary listened to God. She entered deeply into her own heart and pondered God's word to her. And then, ignoring the personal difficulties, she followed where God was leading her even though the journey was beyond improbable. Advent is a time for us to listen, ponder, and recognize the movement of the Spirit in circumstances of our lives.

My time among the poor has shown me the inevitability of the poor getting poorer. But that inevitability stems from our unwillingness to help them help themselves. By what we have done and not done we have added to the storehouse of suffering and indignity.

It seems every film I make and every book I write brings me

closer to the same truth. And that hard truth is this: we need more than an emotional response to the plight of the poor, and we need more than feelings of sorrow and regret. We need to be moved by grace to action. When we hear the cries of the oppressed, the cries of the poor, we hear the voice of God. Where there is weakness, there is God. We need to ask God to shatter our complacency, to strip us of our need for comfort and security.

Mercy, compassion, and love can unite us as a human family, and help us see and know that the poor of Haiti and countless other developing nations are our brothers and sisters, and we must stand with them in fraternity and solidarity. And we can begin to do this by taking at least baby steps toward defying political polarization, consumerism, and militarism and putting our full trust in God's abundance, mercy, and love.

Part of a Whole

Haiti is seared with sadness. The good people of Cité Soleil are stuck in the long, lonely, dark Saturday between the cross and the resurrection, enduring the immensity of waiting for something to change. The change that's needed in Haiti, and in all nations and in all people, needs to emerge from the inside out. External change without an internal change is doomed to failure.

We urgently need to move beyond our individual and nationalistic egos and see ourselves and our countries as part of a whole, each of us living gratefully and contributing to the entire human family, sharing and caring for each out of love.

None of us is entitled to anything. Yet God gives us everything. As angels of compassion we need to commit ourselves to nonviolence and to growing in awareness of the needs of others as we increase our sensitivity to new and better possibilities of serving each other.

In Haiti, the wealth of a few is built upon the poverty of many. The same is true in America. Wall Street gamed and inflated the housing bubble, stealing billions in the process while leaving millions of households in ruin, as countless Americans lost pay, jobs, homes, and savings. We need to return to the principle of the common good.

We can't create a good society on a foundation of maximizing the profits of industry and business and maximizing the choices for consumers, especially when both profit and choice depend on risky and unsustainable levels of corporate and personal debt. Allowing the common good to take primacy in our lives will help us live well together, and will help us create social conditions that will allow everyone to more easily reach their full human potential.

How odd: we seek peace by going to war. How perplexing: we seem unconcerned that well over 10,000 children die every day from hunger, while so many adults are looking for the perfect diet. We can no longer pretend war is an option. We can no longer accept death caused by hunger. That's the kind of change we really need. Perhaps our enemies do not need to be defeated; perhaps our enemies need to be healed. And healing never comes at the point of a gun. In Haiti, healing can begin with a piece of bread. Instead of bread many people in Cité Soleil eat mud cakes.

True and False

A few weeks before leaving for Haiti, I penned the following words in my journal:

> *We live in a constant state of genesis, always changing, always evolving, always being born anew. Today we begin again. This very moment is pregnant with new possibilities for growing in God, with God, through God. Today is a new creation.*

After Haiti, the idea that every moment is pregnant with new possibilities seems both more real and more false at the same time. I am struck with how blessed I am to have the freedom to be present to this very moment, to be aware of the new possibilities grace places before me. What if I lived in Cité Soleil, and I woke up in the mud, had a lunch consisting of mud cakes, spent every moment fighting hunger and despair, had to defecate in a pile of rotting garbage? Would I be able to see the day as a new creation, a gift of God? I doubt it.

In the foreboding, postapocalyptic landscape of Cité Soleil, a woman dressed in rags bends down and embraces a child. And this simple act of love brightens the darkness of this distressing place. In the Incarnation, God bends down to embrace us in love. And in that gentle, unending love each day is a new creation.

Lift Up Your Eyes

On my first trip to Haiti, I was accompanied by my assistant, Jeremy Seifert, a graduate of Fuller Theological Seminary in Pasadena, California. What caught our attention the most in Cité Soleil were the kids, who had not yet been robbed of their joyful innocence and creative ability to make toys out of rubbish. In a film we did in Uganda, Jeremy often shared on camera what he was feeling as we witnessed the extremes of poverty. I asked him if he would pen a few words for this book about his experience in Haiti in December.

> *What helped me get through the ineffable devastation of Cité Soleil were the kites. Before I noticed them late in the afternoon, I had*

not once lifted my eyes from the trash and mud and sewage sprawling before me. Every sense pulls on you for attention because each element in front of you cannot be categorized or properly understood. The children barefoot in heaps of trash, pigs nestled within the garbage and grunting next to a young mother defecating in the open, creaking tin leaned together for a family's home, an animal stench mixed with death. You cannot look away. You feel it all around you, and every sensation becomes over-loaded, paralyzing and silencing you. To keep walking and filming you must resist the need to process everything assaulting your physical body, your emotions, your spirit.

But in the midst of this gutted landscape of a forgotten people, an onshore breeze sweeps clean, salty air into the fetid heat, and makeshift kites lift into the air. Many defy physics with their shoe-strings and crooked sticks fitted awkwardly round a torn plastic bag. Maybe an angel is assigned to each little child's handmade kite to keep it afloat for a brief moment of laughter, to lift eyes from the muck underfoot. Other kites soar high with unbelievable octagonal designs, little works of art tugging at the countless pieces of cloth and rope knotted into a hundred-foot kite string. In the mud, cir-cles of bare feet crowd around the older boy who has designed the kite that makes it high above the corrugated roofs and black smoke of Cité Soleil. Down the way, by a burning pile of trash, a tiny girl pulls on a five-foot string tied to a black plastic bag. She runs in short bursts and turns to see if her kite is flying, bringing it back down to the ground with each stop. She looks sad playing alone, but maybe she is just hungry, and probably sick like many children in the slum. I rushed toward these kites when I first saw them. There was an immediate draw to them, like something I could finally understand in an indefinable place.

Children with kites is something I have seen; it is human and I needed that connection in what felt like an inhuman setting. I filmed the kites dancing and bobbing in the Caribbean breeze, and I filmed all the children laughing at the end of the string, eyes fixed on the kite. The string holds the kite down, keeping the tension against the wind so it can fly above the stolid half-life of poverty . . . but not too far above it. These were children at play in a nightmare, and it afforded me the chance to look up, to see beauty, untainted by all the injustice that creates a slum. A single kite about to break apart in the breeze and surrounded by infinite blue put a big smile on my face, and I began laughing with all the smiling faces surrounding me.

Garbage shaped by imagination and the instinct for play into a work of art that flies! This is what we have to learn from children. This is the endurance and humanness of an innocent life that insists on living beyond mere survival, and transcends the groveling and bitterness that such injustice should incite. I'll have to leave all the deeper connections and implications within this metaphor to serious theologians . . . the kite soaring in rich blue sky above the madness, and the tenuous, yet grounded, connection of the string held by filthy fingers. The beauty and joy found when we become like little children. And the screaming imperative that we must see these children as our own, and fight for them to live and to play as if we were struggling for our own lives.

Catchers

Henri Nouwen, the celebrated spiritual writer and priest from the Netherlands whose personal spiritual journey brought him from teaching at the University of Notre Dame, Yale, and Harvard to living in community with the developmentally disabled, had a fascination with circus trapeze artists. He was struck by their courage and how the fliers lived dangerously, dancing in air, until they were caught by the strong hands of their partners, the catchers. He saw their performances as a true feat of trust.

Father Nouwen wrote: "Before they are caught, they must let go. They must brave the emptiness of space. Living with this kind of willingness to let go is one of the great challenges we face. Whether it concerns a person, possession, or personal reputation, in so many areas we hold on at all costs. We become heroic defenders of our dearly gained happiness. We treat our sometimes inevitable losses as failures in the battle for survival. The great paradox is that it is in letting go, we receive. We find safety in unexpected places of risk. And those who try to avoid risk, those who would try to guarantee that their hearts will not be broken, end up in a self-created hell."

It was something about letting go and being caught that captured Nouwen's attention. The flying trapeze artists became a powerful metaphor for the spiritual life, one that was especially useful to reassure those who were dying. Nouwen said, "Dying is trusting the catcher."

For the people of Cité Soleil, there is no catcher. They are in free fall toward premature death. We need to become their catchers, holding out our hands, and in doing so, our limited and very conditional love becomes a conduit for God's unlimited and unconditional love to touch and heal the people of Cité Soleil.

Becoming catchers of the poor requires a deeper understanding of compassion.

Nouwen wrote: "Jesus' compassion is characterized by a downward pull. That is what disturbs us. We cannot even think about ourselves in terms other than an upward pull, upward mobility in which we strive for better lives, higher salaries, and more prestigious positions. Thus, we are deeply disturbed by a God who embodies a downward movement. Jesus' whole life and mission involved accept-

ing powerlessness and revealing in this powerlessness the limitless love of God. Here we see what compassion means. It is not bending toward the under-privileged from a privileged position; compassion means going directly to those people and places where suffering is most acute and building a home there."

Wow . . . that's really a tough message. But if I really think about it, that is the message of Christmas. God became the child of a refugee couple forced to give birth in a barn surrounded by animals. That is downward mobility at its zenith. I don't mind coming to Cité Soleil for a week, but I can't imagine living there. Perhaps that is because I still can't grasp the full ramification of the fact that the cross is the intersection of love and suffering.

The Human Suffering Index

Paul Farmer is a professor of Medical Anthropology at Harvard Medical School. He has worked as a physician in rural Haiti for twenty-five years fighting the most difficult diseases under the most adverse conditions. He is the founding director of Partners in Health. In his book *Pathologies of Power: Health, Human Rights, and the New War on the Poor,* Dr. Farmer writes:

Working in contemporary Haiti, where in recent decades political violence has added to the worst poverty in the hemisphere, one learns a great deal about suffering. In fact, the country has long constituted a sort of laboratory for the study of affliction, no matter how it is defined. "Life for the Haitian peasant of today," observed the anthropologist Jean Weise some thirty years ago, "is abject misery and a rank familiarity with death." The biggest problem, of course, is unimaginable poverty, as a long succession of dictatorial governments has been more engaged in pillaging than in protecting the rights of workers, even on paper. As Eduardo Galeano noted in 1973, at the height of the Duvalier dictatorship, "The wages Haiti requires by law belong in the department of science fiction: actual wages on coffee plantations vary from $.07 to $.15 a day."

In some sense, the situation has worsened since. When in 1991 international health and population experts devised a "human suffering index" by examining several measures of human welfare ranging from life expectancy to political freedom, 27 of 141 countries were characterized by "extreme human suffering." Only one of them, Haiti, was located in the Western hemisphere. In only three countries on earth was suffering judged to be more extreme than that endured in Haiti; each of these three countries was in the midst of an internationally recognized civil war.

Suffering is certainly a recurrent and expected condition in Haiti's Central Plateau, where everyday life has felt, often enough, like war. "You get up in the morning," observed one young widow with four children, "and it's a fight for food and wood and water."

The Poverty of Humanity

Why is there so much suffering? Why are so many people neglected? How can such widespread misery exist?

Questions, questions, questions.

There are an abundance of questions in Haiti, but answers are rare and seem feeble. Haitians and well-intentioned outsiders are quick to offer an array of social, economic, and political ideas rising out of the questions. But nothing changes, and the misery goes on virtually unabated. The reality of so much suffering should deeply disturb us and render us mute.

Yet in the chaos, confusion, and reeking garbage, a gentle smile, a tender touch, or a child flying a paper plate kite breaks through the anguish and anger . . . and the heart of God is revealed. In these sweet moments it is as if God humbly bends low to kiss a child on the head or to offer a comforting hand. But these moments of grace are obscured by the coldness of cynicism and the cruelty of greed. Tears wash away smiles. Hopelessness overpowers hope.

Why?

In these sick slums the poverty of humanity is revealed, and our powerlessness is on full display. The potential within each of us as children of God is thwarted by our pettiness, selfishness, and callous indifference.

Dr. Paul Farmer reminds us that "violence and chaos will not go away if the hunger, illness, and racism that are the lot of so many are not addressed in a meaningful and durable fashion."

The slums of Cité Soleil brought me to my knees and kept me there for a long time before I could speak.

The "why" of suffering is an unanswerable question. For reasons beyond our comprehension, God created a world where affliction exists, and the affliction seems random and arbitrary. We prefer seeking a supernatural remedy for suffering, while the life of Christ indicates we should be seeking a supernatural use for suffering.

The depth of our affliction is where we encounter the immensity of God's love.

One Word

Christ loved every human being, without exception, without limits. Can we do otherwise? Love casts out the darkness of hate and division. From love flow understanding, compassion, mercy, forgiveness, and peace. Love unites. Love is One.

Thomas Merton said, "The whole idea of compassion is based on a keen awareness of the interdependence of all these living beings, which are all part of one another and all involved in one another."

God is talking to us. God has always been talking to us. God will always be talking to us. God has been, is, and will be saying one word: Love.

And in that love rests a profound truth: We are one. We just imagine (as Thomas Merton pointed out) that we are not one, that division exists within the human family. In God there is unity. In the beginning, we were one. We are still one. We just need to recover our original unity. At the Last Supper, Jesus prayed that we all may be one. Communion needs to be a significant part of our spiritual syntax. To isolate ourselves from the world stifles our ability to sense the dignity of the divine image in human beings.

The road to salvation is, of course, a journey to wholeness. When people lack the basic necessities to sustain life—clean water, adequate nutrition, essential health care, electricity, and sanitation—it is hard to become whole. Survival is struggle enough. For the people in these slums, their every waking moment is directed toward meeting their basic physical needs.

To see a woman squatting in the rotting rubbish to urinate or defecate is an unthinkable indignity. In love, through love, and with love we must unite and eradicate such indignity wherever it is found. We are called to incarnate God's love. It really is that simple. If we have the will to do it, we will figure out how to do it.

In Such a Filthy Place

Sometimes when I am filming, something totally unexpected happens. In Cité Soleil, I saw a little girl, perhaps five or six years old, walking through the trash. She had on rags, yet she somehow radiated a sense of beauty and innocence. I turned on the video camera and followed her as she walked. Flies and insects were swirling around her. She was not wearing shoes, yet she was walking through trash that had to contain hidden sharp objects. I had no idea where she was going, I just found her image and the gentle way she walked to be compelling, and so I kept the camera rolling as I followed her solitary journey. Suddenly, she stopped, pulled down her shorts, and squatted down to urinate. As soon as I realized what was happening, I quickly panned the camera away to protect her privacy and dignity. But that little girl, walking barefoot through the trash surround-

ed by a host of bugs, on a journey to a quiet spot to pee really disturbed me, deeply upset me. But that is the reality. And we can't hide
from it. This is hard stuff to see, and it forces us to face hard choices as how to respond. There should be no place on earth where an
innocent, little girl should be forced to urinate in such a filthy place
and in such a public manner.

One with All

Christ was born in a world where there was no room for him. His
first earthly home was with people who had no home, people who
were regarded as weak and powerless. Christ belonged to people
who did not belong.

And so, with people for whom there is no room in our world,
Christ is present. And Christ calls us to make our home among
them, to be one with them, to love them as He does.

Not all of us literally need to make our home among the rejected, but all of us need "to be at home" with them, that is to be comfortable among them, to spend time with them, to laugh with them,
to cry with them, to embrace them, to be bound in fraternity with

them, to have them present within us, always mindful of their needs. To be one with God is to be one with all.

The Mystical Flame

We often talk about our sinfulness in terms of blindness, and our redemption in terms of seeing. We are blind to the needs of the poor; we do not want to see their plight. We turn away from the sight of those who endure the pain of living without the basic necessities of life. Heads often turn away from the screen when I show my films in public.

No one wants to see what I am filming in Haiti. I don't want to see it. Because in seeing it, I can't forget it, and I must do something about it. In the very act of reaching out in compassion to others, I discover myself and liberate my false self from the unseen prison of my own ego.

So many people today are weary of consumerist living. Many are also disillusioned with institutional forms of religion. The crisis of belonging so many feel has given rise to a widespread spiritual hunger, a search for the mystical flame that long ago had been consumed by darkness and doubt and materialism.

For me, poverty was the road back to God. I think everyone can benefit from spending time with the poor and with the saintly people who live their lives in service to the poor. They know about poverty and prayer; they can relight the flame of faith.

An ember of faith fanned by the holy breath of God can turn into a blazing fire of love.

A Tender Touch

Christ always approached people in a gentle, humble manner, seeking only to refresh them with a tender touch, a kind word. He always personified the love to which he called others. He gave himself fully to everyone. He saw everyone as a brother and sister, a child of God. He broke down the walls that separate humans from each other.

If we are to be the incarnate body of Christ, we too must love, must give ourselves away, must be with the poor. Our individual welfare cannot be separated from the welfare of those around us.

So much of what passes for compassion these days is little more than condescending piety. Such demeaning compassion often comes dressed as pity, which only shames rather than restores. True compassion stems from fellowship and interdependence. We need to recognize our common humanity and realize God sets a banquet before all of us, to be shared by all of us.

Sharing and Serving

We need each other to become whole. Human convergence comes through love. Love unites what has become fragmented and isolated. And in our unity we still keep our individuality, with each gift of life creating a beautiful particle that helps form the whole of life, the full body of Christ. God is unity.

God pulls us out of our isolation by showering us with the grace to see that our lives and gifts must be put to the service of others and all of creation, because through acts of sharing and serving we shall move toward union. In reaching out to others, including our enemies, we are reaching up to God.

So many people are obsessively concerned about salvation and the afterlife, but for the most part those concerns are merely distractions from this life, where so many are denied access to the basic things required to sustain life here on earth.

More important than salvation and the afterlife is that we love God with the fullness of our attention and love each other as God loves us. When you encounter a hungry person, and out of your love of God give that person something to eat, you have begun to experience salvation in its purest form. The road to authentic salvation is to empty ourselves of all desire except for the desire for God.

Giving and Forgiving

The God whom Jesus reveals is not a God consumed with power, but a God interested in relationships of caring fidelity, a God who is in solidarity with the most vulnerable and most needy.

Jesus gives and forgives. When we walk with Jesus, God's generosity is guaranteed, making greed and the frenetic pursuit of acquiring more and more of everything both inappropriate and unnecessary. Jesus gives us new marching orders: love one another. And in the eyes of Jesus, a brother and a sister is everyone, even those who don't look like us, don't act like us, don't believe like us . . . and even those who make us uncomfortable or hate us.

Jesus calls us to an alternative way of life, a way that says no to control, power, and domination, a way which says yes to trusting in the abundance of God. Our culture and our government certainly do not embrace such a way of life. A fundamental principle of the gospel insists that the weakest and least presentable people are indispensable to the church. Sadly, the church, just like the rest of society, seems more enamored with the wealthy and powerful.

Authentic Wealth

Our society is organized around one goal: to constantly increase production and consumption. In time, this slowly breaks down the cluster of communities which have always made up the human family because we become more and more me-centered, more and more addicted to self-fulfillment, more and more individualistic in our pursuit of more and more consumer goods. Instead of being persons in a community, we have been reduced to individuals in a market.

The more we accumulate, the more we waste. And we are never fulfilled. In the midst of our affluence, we are overworked, exhausted, stressed out, and unsatisfied. We bring our laptop computers with us on vacation so we can work. We drive fast, eat fast food, and are impatient with anything less than the fastest internet connection. We have no time for anything else but the pursuit of more. Enough is never enough. The longing within us is never satisfied by adding to our storehouse of material things. How can we continue to justify our reckless pursuit of comfort and extravagance in the midst of world poverty? The abundant life that God promises has nothing to do with increasing material things. The abundant life that God desires for us creates an authentic wealth by expanding compassion and community.

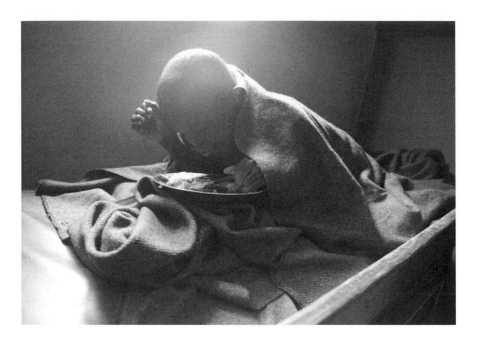

Archbishop Oscar Romero said, "Christ put his classroom of redemption among the poor—not because money is evil, but because money often makes slaves of those who worship the things of earth and forget about God."

The Body of Christ

After spending five hours under the blazing sun documenting the suffering and misery of the people of Cité Soleil, I returned to the hotel. The ordered and ideal world of the hotel, with its overhead fans, neatly set dinner tables, fully stocked bar, fashionable art displays, garden spots, pool, and dependable supply of electricity, stands in stark contrast to the swirling disorder of chaos and confusion of the streets. Uniformed men with powerful rifles guarded the entrance of this locus of decorum and dignity.

I was filthy, and my clothes were wet with perspiration. All I wanted was to take a shower. I became annoyed when I realized that there was no hot water.

And that regrettable fact tells me more about why conditions in Cité Soleil go untreated. Like most people, I am too self-centered to care about anything other than myself. My concern for the poor goes only so far. I am unwilling to lay down my life for the poor.

Life is a challenge. Challenges face everyone, but they are disproportionately overwhelming for the poor. Cité Soleil reflects the divisions and unfairness within all the different societies that make up the global human family.

Saint Paul saw all the difficulties within the community of Corinth, and how indifferent people were to the plight of so many of their neighbors. He suggested that to be part of a community requires one to suffer with those who are suffering. He reminded the people of Corinth, and us also, that they were the Body of Christ, and individually members of it. To be part of a larger body means we can't live on our own or for ourselves. We live instead for the whole body.

Thinking only for ourselves is essentially self-love, which leads to the accumulation of goods for ourselves, without regard for the common good. We need to be as Saint Paul was, living in solidarity with those in need.

The Eyes of Christ

Following Jesus requires a lot more than learning abstract ethical and moral principles; it requires a change in heart, a change in the way we look at life. A heart transformed by the love of Christ is a patient heart, a heart that takes the time to be still and to listen. To see with the eyes of Christ is to see the beauty of all creation, to see the beauty within ourselves and within each other.

We are all in such a hurry, rushing from here to there, from this to that, an endless treadmill of movement going nowhere. Anxiety is as common as a penny. We are anxious about the future, our jobs, our relationships . . . we are anxious about virtually everything. And our anxiety breeds a drive to acquire more and more of everything. Nothing is enough. We want more of everything. More money, more prestige, more clothing, more contacts, better cars, bigger houses, faster computers.

It is in our endless movement, our constant rushing, that we futilely attempt to distract ourselves from our own loneliness, our brokenness. We are all wounded. But as our hearts become more transformed by the presence of Christ, we are able, in our weakness, to feel the love of God and to trust in the abundance of God's love.

Our relentless drive to acquire more is fueled by our deeply rooted sense of scarcity, our desire for self-sufficiency, and our inability to trust that God wants to give us all that we need.

Out of Sight

In Haiti and the many other impoverished nations where I have filmed, such as Uganda and Kenya, the poverty is stunningly clear and all around you. It hits you in the face every day.

Here at home in America, the poverty is more hidden, more out of sight. Still, the drastic unequal distribution of wealth in the United States has reaped consequences that place an added grim burden on the poor, which you can see if you look closely: failed urban schools, crumbling infrastructure, astronomical rates of incarceration among minorities and the poor, unfavorable health outcomes for the insured and uninsured alike, and constant economic insecurity for most of us thanks to failing banks and rising unemployment.

We need to begin to think more seriously about the common good both at home and abroad and better understand that compassion is crucially essential to our survival as individuals and as a society.

A Broken World

In Haiti, it is clear that a sea of graft and corruption is drowning the poor. At home, stealing from the poor is more subtle, but no less painful. We are slow to compassion because we are quick to exploit others for our own gain. We are slow to compassion because of our own misguided sense of scarcity wherein nothing is ever enough because we do not trust the abundance of God. As we grow in compassion we are able to see more clearly the beauty of all life, and we also increase our desire and capacity to transform everything ugly into something beautiful.

Action is as important as prayer; each of us must take responsibility for meeting the world's needs, for we are the accomplices of evil if we do nothing to prevent it. Contemplation and action are flip sides of

the same coin. Contemplation means to witness and respond. At the inception of Christianity, centuries ago, Christ's followers were told, "Let us not love with words or tongue but with actions and in truth." If only this message had been heeded, we'd live in a much different world. But ours is a broken world in turmoil. We need restoration and wholeness. We need to love with actions and in truth. We need Christ.

The creative power of God is in the midst of evil, ever ready to redeem it. God is constantly revealing her transforming, redemptive power. If you are a disciple of Christ, you should be doing the work of Christ. To be a follower of Christ is to be a friend of the poor and the excluded.

Faith should not be locked up in the mind. Faith needs to be lived out—by service to the will of God.

Soup to Salvation

Even though Haiti is not far from the United States, not everyone can go there to lend a helping hand. Most of us can't go to the countless desperate places in Africa that so urgently need our help. But we all can do something right here at home, from busy professionals to stay-at-home mothers to high school students. I can't imagine an American city where there isn't a soup kitchen or mission serving the growing numbers of destitute homeless in the United States. The rising number of homeless families in the wealthiest nation on earth should be deeply disturbing to all Americans.

Serving in a soup kitchen leads us to a tangible experience of being in the presence of God, because service to the poor leads us beyond just thinking about God, into literally being with God in the person of our neighbor. My passion for the poor was born in a soup kitchen in Philadelphia, the St. Francis Inn, which I documented in my film *Room at the Inn*. The act of serving is a sacramental gesture in which we touch a sacred reality here and now. We touch God through serving God's treasured creatures.

When we become aware of the suffering caused by unmindful consumption, we begin to take baby steps toward cultivating more mindful eating, drinking, and consuming. And in practicing this, we have begun an attempt to preserve peace, well-being, and joy in not only our own consciousness but also in the collective body of humanity and the consciousness of society. Moreover, we slowly begin to transform the violence, fear, and anger we find within ourselves and society through acts of healing and peace.

Tear Down Those Walls

There are no walls in Cité Soleil. Yet, in a way, Cité Soleil is all about walls . . . the walls that separate us from each other. Within our society, there are insurmountable walls between the rich and the poor, between the powerful and the weak. Even within ourselves we have erected walls that separate us from our authentic motives and inner selves. The walls between each other and within each of us are constructed out of loneliness and separation from God. Walls are built out of fear; yet Jesus tells us perfect love casts out all fear. The people of Cité Soleil have been pushed aside and are huddled together in a netherworld of injustice and pain. The wall between them and us is virtually impenetrable. But Christ calls us to tear down those walls, and with the help of Christ, the walls between us and within us can come tumbling down and we can live in unity instead of fear. Fear builds walls. Love demolishes walls.

Gospel Giving

As I filmed the people of Cité Soleil, I realized the poverty of my own service to the poor. I question if I am doing enough and wonder what more I could do. I feel overwhelmed and inadequate, becoming increasingly aware of my own poverty and brokenness.

Yet despite the agony I film, I do not sink into despair. I can sense God's grace somehow mysteriously at work within me. I can't explain it, but being in Cité Soleil somehow brings me closer to the heart of God.

Our very woundedness is waiting to be transformed into compassion. Our emotional and physical pain helps us understand and respond to the suffering of one another. Compassion is more elegant than any cathedral constructed by human hands, for it is entering into the very heart of God.

There is a fourfold cycle to a life of worship. We feel some deep need. We cry out to God for help. God responds. We give thanks. And in that repeated cycle our lives are transformed and we begin to look at the world in a very different way. We slowly imagine a different world, a world where God's compassionate presence is fully manifested in us and through us.

We view the world around us, with its spirit of self-indulgence, through the eyes of Christ, and we are able to see things differently from the way our materialistic and militaristic society wishes us to see things. We see, for instance, how we have turned medical care into a commodity that feeds the greed of soulless corporations more concerned about their bottom line than our well-being.

We see how our culture, in blind pursuit of power and greed, has forgotten God. With God removed from our cultural consciousness, we have no need for fidelity to God's relational way; we have no need for thankfulness to a faithful God.

With God gone, neatly put into a box labeled fairy tale or myth (or worse, reduced to a comfortable dogmatic formula), we begin to sink into a cultural sea of self-indulgence. We slowly forget that life

is a gift. We begin to live without a spirit of gratitude. We no longer see a world of abundance; life is reduced to a commodity, a series of market transactions. We even begin to leverage social goods, like medical care and education, into profit centers.

And of course, we no longer hear the plaintive cries of distress from the poor. But God hears, and God is faithful and God responds and makes transformation possible. When we begin to really hear God, we too will hear the cries of the poor and become part of God's mysterious response.

At Easter, we proclaim in song that "Christ is risen." And he truly has. But yet, when we look at the reality of the world around us, we see death and destruction, revenge and retaliation. Our culture of death dominates our spirit of life. We have lost our prophetic voice and we no longer defend the stranger, the widow, and the orphan, those who are hurting and have no voice.

Cité Soleil and places like it exist because we as the human family have forgotten God and turned our backs on God's children.

We need to share our time, our treasure, and our love with the chronically poor. Jesus wants us to give our lives away. This is gospel giving. And as we give of ourselves, God gives God's self to us and we are transformed into sons and daughters in whom God delights, and whom God nourishes and protects.

Fatigue of Compassion

We live in a time of global anxiety. Everyone feels threatened and concerned about the future, which looks more and more bleak for more and more people. Loneliness, fear, and a sense of emptiness have reached epidemic proportions.

There are times in my work among the chronically poor of the world that I'm left with a feeling of hopelessness. We seem to tinker around the edges in our efforts to relieve their suffering, offering little more than speculative comments from afar. We might be willing to give some spare change, but we are not willing to change how we live, to live more simply so others can simply live.

I sense within people a fatigue of compassion. The need is so great that our humble efforts to help seem woefully inadequate. The only way for me to chase away the hopelessness is to spend time in prayer every day. Prayer is a lifeline to hope.

Dropping Band-Aids from an Airplane

As I was preparing for my first trip to Haiti prior to the massive earthquake of January 2010 a journalist friend of mine who had recently spent a few weeks in Haiti said something that shocked me: "Haiti is crawling with good will, with well-intentioned people doing all they can for the poor, yet it seemed like little more than dropping Band-Aids from an airplane."

He went on to describe how primitive virtually everything was. Normal infrastructure was nonexistent. Endless chaos was the order of the day. He said conditions such as those he encountered are usually seen after a natural disaster or a prolonged war, but even then only sections of a country would be really bad off. In Haiti, he said, the disaster is all pervasive; you see it everywhere you go.

He also noted an extreme individualism within the people. Self-interest trumps all else in the lives of most Haitians. Virtually everyone from national politicians to the people in the slums is out for himself or herself. Everything is "me first," he said, because everything is about personal survival. For many Haitians, there is no long-term picture. There is so much chaos, people can't hold onto anything about the future.

My time in Haiti before Christmas confirmed everything my friend said . . . and more. Just one day with Father Tom could make your head spin. He has paid a huge price for trying to bring relief to the desperate people of Cite Soleil. In his sixteen years in the slum, more than twenty of his staff and volunteers were murdered.

The social fabric in the slums of Port-au-Prince consists of layers of opposing forces. Daily life is dominated by duplicity, fear, ambition, jealousy, rivalry, rumor, false perceptions, slander, and, to make things even more dangerous, a current of violence that flows just beneath the surface of it all. Nothing happens without a vast network of people spreading news and rumors. Some of the details of the violence are too gruesome to repeat. The fact that Father Tom's previous dog was set on fire and killed gives a hint of the brutality.

Haiti is a dark place, and it is tempting to say, as I have, that it is hopeless. But the light did come into the world and the darkness cannot extinguish it—therefore, there is always hope, perhaps a timid and fragile hope, but hope exists whenever one person reaches out to another in a spirit of compassion and genuine human kindness.

It is the imperfection, the crack, the flaw in everything and everyone, that lets the light in.

Tragedy upon Tragedy

Gerald A. Drew, the former U.S. ambassador to Haiti (1957–1960), once said: "In Haiti, I believe nothing I hear, and only half of what I see." Even by that hard-nosed standard, everything about Haiti screams scarcity. There is a scarcity of food, clean water, and electricity. There is a scarcity of jobs and pocket money. There is a scarcity of education, health care, and technology. There is a scarcity of comfort and safety. There is a scarcity of mercy and truth. There is a scarcity of possibilities. And saddest of all, there is a scarcity of hope and dreams. And this inescapable, all-pervasive reality of scarcity existed before the earthquake.

The history of Haiti offers countless clues why and how this island nation came to be as it is today, a country badly broken, virtually dysfunctional, and deeply wounded by widespread corruption, constant political upheaval, military coups, unthinkable violence, rampant hunger, and a bankrupt government. Even a broad-stroke look at Haiti's history helps put the situation that existed before the earthquake in context. The history of Haiti reads like a sorrowful litany of tragedy upon tragedy, a long line of slaughter and assassinations, revolts and coups, despots and dictators, repression and cruelty.

Nestled on the forested, western end of the island of Hispaniola, Haiti has been the scene of almost unrelieved heartache since it was spotted by Columbus in 1492. Within a century, the rapacious Spanish colonists had slaughtered the original inhabitants. After Haiti was ceded to France, it became the richest colony in the Americas, though nine-tenths of its people were destitute slaves. After a slave revolt, Haiti became, in 1804, the second American nation to gain independence. A line of despots ensued, and revolts against them; in 1915 the U.S. Marines entered Haiti and began the U.S. occupation of the country. The United States rewrote the Haitian constitution and ensured that only Haitian politicians who supported our economic interests rose to the presidency. Only in the 1940s did Washington call the Marines home and cede control.

François Duvalier, elected in 1957 thanks to U.S. backing, turned Haiti into a police state that he ruled until his death in 1971. Duvalier's rise to power put an end to a century-long period when Haiti's mulatto elite, with U.S. help, ran the country. The dark-skinned Duvalier rode a tidal wave of black power into the presidency. Then he used the office to fatten his own bank account while impoverishing the nation. For fourteen years he ruled like an old-fashioned, iron-fisted dictator, killing anyone who opposed him. And to punctuate his point, he often left the corpses on the street corner. He even killed entire families by locking them in their homes and then setting the house on fire. His vast network of exceedingly violent thugs was a menacing force feared by everyone. The Kennedy administration gave Duvalier financial aid to help build an airport in exchange for Haiti's vote to expel Cuba from the Organization of American States (OAS). Noam Chomsky notes, "Kennedy also provided the bloodthirsty killer with military assistance as part of a general program of extending U.S. control over the security forces in Latin America."

As he approached death, Papa Doc, as he was known, bequeathed the country to his bungling nineteen-year-old son, Jean-Claude Duvalier, who was dubbed Baby Doc. The son ruled in the same cruel and corrupt manner as his father for fifteen years, until he was overthrown and forced to flee the country on February 7, 1986, aboard a U.S. cargo plane that also carried Baby Doc's BMW. During twenty-nine years of rule, the Duvaliers ignited unparalleled Haitian-on-Haitian violence. They amassed a vast fortune for themselves and left the nation deeply in debt and completely impoverished. As Jean-Claude and his family winged their way to France, the Haitians began to loot and destroy every building associated with the father and son's back-to-back reign of terror. In a furious attempt to expunge Duvalierism from their system, they smashed furniture and set files on fire. And they also slaughtered some of the Duvaliers' associates.

After an interregnum, the army took over, promising reform but delivering repression. In 1990, Jean-Bertrand Aristide, a populist Catholic priest and charismatic champion of the poor, won the first free and fair democratic election in the country's history. Sadly, Aristide was not immune to the negative temptations of power and employed bullying tactics that engendered mistrust among Haiti's elite. Aided by foreign meddling, the military soon ousted Aristide. International condemnation led to a trade embargo, concessions by coup leaders, the reneging on the concessions, and renewed embargoes. Aristide managed to regain the presidency, but his second term also was short-lived, and he now lives in exile with his wife in South Africa. Aristide was followed by the current president, René Préval, a passive, ineffectual leader who seems to be sleepwalking his way through the job. In the aftermath of the earthquake he has been living in a tent virtually missing in action.

Haiti's history gives little reason for optimism.

Haiti's problem, at its core, is the tragic outcome of perhaps the most heinous racism the world has ever known. What began as an innocent landing in 1492 turned genocidal as the Tainos Indians died from European diseases such as smallpox introduced by the Spanish for which they had no immunity. Then, the Spanish killed off the remaining native population and began importing Africans as slaves. The newly arrived slaves were overwhelmed and horrified by the brutal working conditions. Under the heavy burden of back-breaking work and disease, they died by the thousands and were simply replaced by boatloads of fresh slaves who would in turn be ground into submission and death.

In time, Spain ceded the island's western third to France, and kept what is today's Dominican Republic. The French took over where the Spanish left off and treated the slaves worse. Slave labor produced enormous wealth for France, providing nearly half of France's gross national product. The slaves produced 60 percent of all Europe's coffee and 40 percent of all Europe's sugar. The French could not build ships fast enough to transport fresh slaves to replace those who had been worked to death in the fields harvesting the sugar or in the wood-burning refining factories. Most slaves never lived long enough to see their fortieth birthday. By the 1780s, Haiti was importing 40,000 new slaves a year. Because Africa could not meet France's ferocious appetite for slaves, slaves were purchased or kidnapped from nearby Jamaica and from Louisiana. The French used extreme barbarity to control the salves. A slacker slave would be buried up to his neck, doused in molten sugar, and left for insects to devour. The thought of such a torturous death kept the slaves working past exhaustion. Eventually, the slaves revolted. Fueled by pent-up anger over years of mistreatment and abuse, they retaliated by punishing the French measure for measure, unleashing a tsunami of torture, brutal dismemberment, and slaughter of women and children, businessmen and community leaders. The hell that was already Haiti only deepened after that first massacre of the French by the black slaves, as the oppressed became the oppressor. Humanity seems blind to the reality that returning evil for evil leaves no room for reconciliation.

The story only continues a cycle of crime and punishment, with each spin bleaker and more heinous than the one before. It is the darkest history of any nation on earth.

Haiti was born and bred in hatred, oppression, deprivation, and despair. Empires came and went, flourished by exploiting that small island parcel, once paradise, today hell. Abandoned finally by its colonial parents who had abused it since its birth, too spent, too exhausted, too long oppressed, completely without any resources, with barely a glimmer of a vision of who it could be among its brother and sister island nations, or in the world, this spot of soil, like a small metastasizing boil on the earth, turned into a villainous, rapacious, seething time bomb, awaiting a match.

The poor of Haiti have been maligned, forgotten, and neglected for so long it seems it has taken nothing short of a cataclysmic earthquake claiming more than 200,000 lives for the world to focus on this tormented parcel of humanity and become aware of the torturous conditions so many endured before the earthquake, which has resulted in an outpouring of compassion beyond anything the Haitians have ever before experienced. Out of so much death and destruction, something beautiful emerged . . . people reaching out to people, countless hands reaching out to help those in dire need.

Part II

During the Earthquake Emergency

Signs and Omens

I make films, yet I don't actually think of myself as a filmmaker. My photography has been published and praised, yet I don't think of myself as a photographer. I have written five published books, one of which garnered two prestigious writing awards, yet I don't really think of myself as an author. I'm the head of a nonprofit charitable organization, yet that is not who I am. About twenty times a year, I speak in public, at churches and schools, yet it is something that makes me feel very uncomfortable. And because of all these things I "do," I am usually given instant respect, though I feel unworthy of any special recognition. People generously support financially my efforts to chronicle the plight of the poor on film, which always amazes and humbles me.

Who am I? Why do I do what I do?

In truth, I am just a lost soul, a simple pilgrim trying to find my way back home, back to God. For reasons I truly do not understand, I stumbled onto using my pen and camera as navigational tools to help me enter into the heart of reality, the heart of God. Along the road, I try to pay attention to the little things, unseen moments of grace, that might be showing me a better route. I think it was just one of those grace-filled moments in a church in Pasadena that put me on the road to Haiti, virtually moments before a catastrophic event altered forever the life of that nation, putting me at the epicenter of suffering and compassion. I think most people want to be better able to discern the "signs and omens" in their life that may help them better navigate their way through life, through the valley of disappointment and doubts we all traverse from time to time. How do we know that this person or that job is right for us?

When I set out to make a film or write a book, what is it that is fueling me? I want to be in the center of God's will for me, yet sometimes that is hard to discern. It is easy to mix my motives with God's motives. People do it all the time, pretending they know God's will on a wide range of subjects, everything from how we treat homosexuals, women, and people of other faiths, to what we eat and how we dress.

I work hard at preserving a quiet inner space where I hope from time to time I may faintly hear the silent voice of God. And in this inner sanctuary, poor as it is, God seems always to be calling me to deeper levels of self-emptying and at the same time reaching out to those whose lives are empty of all the essential physical and emotional things needed for human life. So many people live lives of quiet desperation, lives untouched by genuine mercy and compassion.

My thinking that God led me to Haiti does not necessarily make it so. There is a prayer penned by Thomas Merton (in *Thoughts in Solitude*) that beautifully touches on this. "My Lord God, I have no idea where I am going. I do not see the road ahead of me. I cannot know for certain where it will end. Nor do I really know myself, and the fact that I think I am following your will does not mean that I am actually doing so. But I believe that the desire to please You does in fact please You. And I hope I have that desire in all that I am doing. I hope that I will never do anything apart from that desire. And I know that, if I do this, You will lead me to the right road, though I may know nothing about it."

Within hours of the earthquake, I knew I needed to return to Haiti as soon as possible. I had no idea how hard it was going to be to get in to Port-au-Prince. But, through a seemingly miraculous series of events, plans were firmed up for me and my assistant to leave for Haiti via Florida on Thursday night (January 14), just two days after the earthquake.

The earthquake hit Haiti on Tuesday afternoon (January 12). As the hours rolled on, the tragedy intensified. The initial news reports and images were horrifying. By Tuesday, the world was beginning to understand the extent of the damage and the horrific loss of life. Port-au-Prince had been leveled, completely destroyed, and perhaps 100,000 people were crushed in collapsed buildings. We scrambled to catch a flight to Haiti on Tuesday night only to learn that the airport was damaged and closed.

On Tuesday, I was glued to news reports. As my heart became overwhelmed with sadness, I felt I had to return. But how? And was it necessary? Would it do any good?

As I was falling asleep Tuesday night, Danny came to my mind. Back in the late 1990s I was in Albany, New York, making a film about a saintly priest who cared for ex-convicts who were drug addicts. Danny was in the priest's rehab center, fresh out of prison. His recovery was very raw and fragile. Some felt he would slip back into his old ways. I interviewed him on camera, and he was mesmerizing. He said that he used to think that anyone who would steal from their mother in order to get money for a fix was "a piece of shit." Then he looked straight into the camera and said, "Well, I stole from my mother."

It was a sincere and powerful revelation. I asked Danny if he had ever asked his mother for forgiveness. He had not. I learned his mother lived about an hour away, in a trailer park, where she cared for her very ill second husband. I suggested to Danny that we visit her. The priest felt Danny was too new in his recovery to leave the center, but he gave us permission anyway. We filmed Danny hugging his mother and saying he was sorry. You could see the love in her eyes. It was a truly wonderful moment. We then took Danny down to Harlem and he told us on camera standing in front of a tenement crack house how he used to shoot up dope in the building. He spoke graphically about the rats and the naked people . . . and those who died. It was gripping; the intensity of addiction was palpable. Danny's recovery stuck. He has been clean and sober for more than eleven years. He stayed in occasional contact with me over the years, once actually visiting in person when he was in L.A. He said how important that day with me was in his life.

As I lay in bed that Tuesday, unable to sleep because of all the haunting images on the news from Haiti, I remembered that Danny had been working for years at a company that chartered private jets. First thing Wednesday morning, I e-mailed Danny. Within minutes he responded, saying he would see what he could do. A few hours later, Danny wrote to say it was not looking good. Although the single runway at the airport in Port-au-Prince was open, the control tower was badly damaged and not functioning. All commercial flights were canceled, and only humanitarian flights could land. Danny said some pilots did not want to fly into Haiti, and the others were booked solid by high-priced news organizations from around the world.

I called Danny and told him I had to get to Haiti and asked him to really try hard to find me something. He promised he would. Around three o'clock Danny called. He found a small, six-seated jet that could depart from Miami on Friday at noon. Elatedly I asked how much it would cost. He said $12,000. I gulped. During the day my friend Karl Holtsnider from Holy Family Catholic Church in South Pasadena called to say he could raise some funds for my return flight to Haiti if I found a plane. Karl's church is very active in supporting Father Tom Hagan. I guessed Karl might be able to raise a few grand, but $12,000 was out of the question.

Then Danny said something that took the wind out of my sails. He said all the pilot could do is land in Port-au-Prince, drop us off on the runway, and then return to Miami. That sounded reasonable. Then I said, "And he will come back for us in five days." Danny said, "No." It quickly dawned on me that the twelve grand was for a one-way flight. Danny explained we would be charged $3,000 an hour. It was a nearly a two-hour flight and so with the plane's trip back to Miami, we had to pay for four hours, which included a little time for the pilot to clear customs in Miami.

Hopes for returning were quickly fading. I had to raise $12,000 very, very quickly. If I was successful, I would land in Haiti Friday afternoon. I would have no place to stay, no ground transportation, and would only be able to eat and drink whatever food or water we could carry with us. We would, most likely, have to walk wherever we went. We would be essentially on the streets with the tens of thousands of homeless Haitians. Dead bodies were already piling up in the streets. We would be walking into a true nightmare, a living hell, with no real plan on how to get out.

Yet, I was willing to go. I actually wanted to go.

I wrote some people an e-mail, telling them I had found a charter, but it cost $12,000 just to get to Haiti. I said I was leaving the entire thing in the Lord's hands. If the money came by Thursday morning, I would book the charter and trust all would work out, including a flight back to Miami. Within two hours, two people wrote. One pledged $12,000, another $1,000.

I talked to my assistant, Jeremy. We decided to walk through the door that was opening for us. I left work at 6:30 p.m., and as I walked to my car, a line from one of my films dashed across my mind: "Christ is not looking for our spare change, Christ wants our lives." I thought about the deeper meaning of those words.

When I got home, I was horrified by the fresh video coming from the networks. The damage and extent of the catastrophe was suddenly stunningly clear. And just as suddenly, I was confronted with the reality that in less than twenty-four hours I would be in the middle of the chaos, in the middle of all that death and destruction. Jeremy and I spoke on the phone for a while, talking about some practical matters. How much could we carry? We figured we would pretty much just wear the same clothes for five days. How would we get around? We tried to imagine ourselves in the situation we knew existed in Port-au-Prince. We figured we could last for five days on little sleep and little food and water. But getting out was a problem. Could we simply trust we would find a seat on a plane?

As I sat alone on Wednesday night sipping some wine and watching CNN, I became scared. I did not want to see what I would see. I began to cry. I had a hard time falling asleep. Images of the desperately hard life we captured in Cité Soleil in December haunted me. I woke up at 4:00 a.m., and my head was spinning with details of all that had to be done before the flight at 9:00 p.m. And then I thought about the reality we would be facing, the harshness of life in Port-au-Prince. I wanted to get up and call the whole thing off, and return in a few weeks when things had calmed down and just film some collapsed buildings. But how could I truly tell the story of the suffering in Haiti if I could not see, smell, feel, and touch the scope of the disaster? I had to truly be connected with the people, to be one with them in their hour of need. I called Danny and finalized the charter flight.

Overnight more support for our impending, quickly arranged, return trip arrived while I was sleeping. A man in St. Louis pledged a thousand dollars, and Holy Family Church in South Pasadena promised to send $12,000. Exactly what I needed for a chartered flight to get me out of Port-au-Prince following five days of filming the devastation wrought by the earthquake. I couldn't believe it. In less than twelve hours of my appeal for help in funding a chartered flight in and out of Haiti, I had received $26,000 in pledges. Enough to cover the cost of the charter flights and the flights from L.A. to Fort Lauderdale, Florida.

On Tuesday afternoon I had said to myself, "Lord, if you open the door, I will walk through it." Clearly, the door to Haiti was open. I was ready to go even though I really didn't want to see what I knew I would see. Dead babies and young children. People with mangled limbs. And the smell, the noxious smell, of decaying flesh. And the sound, the piercing sound, of people screaming in fear and pain.

But almost as quickly as the plans were made, they slowly began to unravel.

Early Thursday morning, I received a phone call from Karl Holtsnider. The call had good news but yet perplexing news. Father Tom and Doug (the executive of Hands Together who was visiting Haiti), who had not been heard from for days, had made it out of Haiti and into the Dominican Republic where they would be catching a flight back to the States. The main part of my trip, my mission to Haiti, was to find Father Tom and Doug, to capture their experiences of the earthquake on film. All we knew thus far was that the house where Father Tom lived had collapsed, and he had been hit on the head with falling debris but that the injury was minor and he would be okay. At least four Oblate volunteers were buried in the rubble of the home, but unfortunately only two could be dug out alive. Before this news came, Doug's wife e-mailed, practically pleading with me to get her word if I found Doug. I wrote her saying I would find him, even if I had to walk from the airport to Cité Soleil, and, more important, there would be room on the charter flight to bring him home.

Oddly enough, the happy fact that they were not only safe but on their way home posed a little bit of a dilemma. I felt it was still important to film the massive slum of Cité Soleil and the destroyed schools and Father Tom's home. This would be very important in helping Hands Together raise funds to rebuild. I asked Karl if the news about Father Tom and Doug diminished the desire to fund my trip. He said no, that the trip was still important.

Early morning news on the networks and the internet showed

even more clearly the full extent of the damage, with perhaps as many as 100,000 people killed. Port-au-Prince was teetering on the verge of anarchy. There was hardly any rule of law before the earthquake, and during the earthquake the main prison collapsed, freeing all the criminals who were suddenly roaming the streets, hungry and probably willing to do anything for food. I had hoped that the earthquake would give rise to a new understanding of the importance of the common good. This disaster was not the result of political corruption or unbridled greed. It was nature forcefully showing us the fragility of life. However, the extent of the damage can be traced to a severe human failure, as most of the buildings were poorly constructed and the government had no search-and-rescue plan in place. And now the streets, cluttered with homeless people, were becoming more and more dangerous. Chaos was the order of the day.

There were a few voices being gently raised among my family and friends, suggesting that going back to Haiti at this perilous time was not a good idea. I kind of smirked to myself, thinking they figured I wasn't listening and nothing was going to stop me from going. But I was listening. And I was also listening to my heart, and my heart ached to return. Sure, I was frightened and concerned about my safety and what I would see. But I was going to be on the plane to Ft. Lauderdale at 9:00 p.m. no matter what.

When I got to work, Danny called saying there was bad news. The runway was closed. It was cluttered with so much unloaded cargo that planes couldn't land. Worse yet, the airport had run out of fuel, and many of the larger cargo planes that could not be refueled were stuck on the runway. I told Danny not to worry. I was leaving at 10:00 at night; I'd be in Florida at 5:00 in the morning, and by the time of the scheduled departure at noon, those runways would be cleared. They had to be. People were dying. And people from around the world were trying to send in aid. And so, we just continued as if it would all work out.

My friend John Dear, S.J., called, and he told me that Bill Clinton would be landing in Haiti on Friday. I just smiled because I knew the runway would be cleared for him. And we'd just quietly slip in after the former president landed. It was all going to work out. I was supposed to be in Haiti. (Note: Bill Clinton arrived in Haiti on Monday;

Secretary of State Hillary Clinton paid a brief visit to Port-au-Prince on Saturday.)

Sometime around noon I told Jeremy about Father Tom and Doug working their way home. A puzzled look crossed Jeremy's face. It seemed to him that with their departure the dynamics of our trip had been dramatically altered. We then entered into a pretty serious discussion of why we were going and the dangers we faced. We really looked at it from every angle possible. One of our biggest concerns was how we would get around, carrying the cameras, our personal effects, blank tapes and batteries, plus the water and food we'd have to have with us for survival. If Father Tom were there perhaps we'd have access to a vehicle and also someone from his staff who could accompany us through Cité Soleil. With his not being there we would be truly on our own now with no real contact or agenda. I felt this deep need to be one with the suffering people of Haiti, to see their anguish, to feel their pain. I felt my being there in Haiti's darkest hour would help me connect more emotionally to their plight. I felt we would film people differently than the network cameras would, and that I could express myself on camera more powerfully because I was right in the middle of the horror.

We looked deeply into the necessity of our actually being there. It was difficult to imagine exactly how we would survive in the middle of such an unstable situation. The entire trip was a leap into the unknown, and we had no safety net. (The poor people of Haiti never had a safety net.) We were just two guys with a couple thousand dollars in our pockets and a couple of very expensive cameras walking through a population deeply wounded, hungry, and desperate. And yet we came to the conclusion that we had to go. I felt it was necessary, not only for my film, but for my soul.

And then, another call came from Holy Family Church. They were very concerned about the instability in Port-au-Prince. They felt the situation was a powder keg ready to explode in rioting and violence, as the desperate people reacted to the slowness of any response from the government or the outside world. And so they had reached the conclusion that in good conscience they could no longer support the funding of my return flight. I practically pleaded with them, saying how vitally important that trip was. But they kept repeating their concerns, which were unquestionably legitimate. In the end, I told them I understood their reasoning for withdrawing support, and I thanked them for their original interest in helping me charter a flight. I ended by telling them I was going.

It seemed by the hour internet news reports grew grimmer. The debate about going or not going took on a new dimension as we were now $12,000 short. I still felt we had to move forward trusting that either the money would come or I would dip into some of our limited operating funds. Jeremy and I continued to question and debate the decision to go, continued to look at it from every possible angle. I heard the concerns, and I heard my heart. I was also concerned about Jeremy's safety. I even thought about whether or not I could go by myself, but quickly realized that was just not possible, too much stuff for an old man to lug. I decided the prudent course of action was to seek the counsel of a few wise people. I wrote down a list of seven names and began to call. One person after another urged caution, urged me not to go.

Slowly, my strong yes was turning into a weak no. Maybe it would be better to buy some of the disaster aftermath footage and wait a few weeks before returning to Haiti. Wait until some of the roads have been cleared, some order has been established by military units from around the world, and the people have been fed and given clean water. Maybe in a few weeks we'll see something different than bleeding and mangled bodies. We'll see the loneliness of poverty. We'll see the effects of endless waiting for absolutely everything. We'll see the torment of not being able to help yourself.

Around 4:30 p.m. I made one last call . . . to Danny. He all but pleaded with me, in very colorful language, not to go. He had spoken to some Haitians and some airport workers in the Dominican Republic, and they painted a rather brutal picture. He said, "Hey, I never thought this was a good idea. But I figured you go with God and if you wanted to go to Haiti, I would get you there."

By five o'clock Thursday night, a scant two hours before the taxi was scheduled to take Jeremy and me to LAX, I was exhausted from thirteen hours of nonstop thinking about the trip, questioning it, debating it, analyzing it. It was getting too late to go home and pack in time for the scheduled taxi pickup. I had to make a decision. I took a deep breath, and pulled the plug on the return trip. I didn't like doing it. But I listened to the wise and reasonable voices, and probably will always wonder if I should have gone at that time.

Signs and omens. Before heading home, Jeremy and I sat for a little while talking about the lessons from the biblical story of Abraham and Isaac as we tried to discern God's will regarding the return trip to Haiti. At first the signs pointed to going, and then the signs pointed to not going. Tom Roberts shared a brilliant quote from Daniel Berrigan, S.J.: "Our lives are the mysterious intersection of freedom, God's and our own." I think the fact that I was willing to go, willing to follow where I thought the Lord was leading me, was enough, as it was enough that Abraham was willing to sacrifice his son Isaac. The door opened and I was willing to walk through it. But when the door closed, there was no need to bang my head against it. Still, I went home and felt a deep emptiness about not going to Haiti. I believed I was supposed to be there and trusted God would open up a less crazy path back.

Over the following weekend my heart yearned to return to Haiti. On Tuesday morning (January 19) I expressed my desire to a friend who is well connected in the international world of humanitarian services. I told him I had to get back and that waiting for a few weeks was not an option. He contacted an agency that coordinates the efforts of international medical missionaries, and amazingly within thirty minutes I received word that on Thursday (January 21) at three in the morning there was a chartered flight to Port-au-Prince leaving Dallas with twenty-two doctors and nurses and a large amount of medical supplies . . . and there was one open seat which I could have. My only hesitancy was that I didn't think I could do what I had to do by myself . . . there was just too much equipment to carry around and film at the same time. But I quickly brushed that concern aside and found a Wednesday afternoon (January 20) flight to Dallas.

Lies and Deception

After a week of nonstop earthquake coverage, the night before I left for my second trip to Haiti another story was screaming for attention, and Haiti was suddenly competing with Massachusetts for the media's fickle embrace. In a stunning upset, the Republican candidate in the special election to fill Ted Kennedy's senate seat won, perhaps in part because he never used the word "Republican" during his entire campaign. This was a major news story, because with the unexpected Republican victory, health care reform was now in serious jeopardy as the Democrats had lost their sixty-vote supermajority in the United States Senate. (Thanks to silly filibuster rules, a cranky minority in the Senate can thwart the will of the majority.) Earthquake stories from Haiti now split screen time with instant analysis of the impending catastrophic failure of health care reform. I was glad I was going to Haiti, as I could not have endured the endless heated political analysis.

In American politics, honest debate has been replaced by mindless, toxic partisanship where each side uses lies and deception to tarnish the opposition . . . leaving us with legislative gridlock. Politics has degenerated into a frustrating battle of nasty, shouting monologues . . . a Roman coliseum culture where the extremes of both major parties battle each other without listening. Dialogue is no longer possible because we have lost the art of deep listening and the willingness to see the good in our opponents. And in the process we have created a society where no one trusts anyone, and where there is no respect, no civility, and no dialogical listening middle where we can live. Follow political news for one week and it will become clear that we have developed an aversion to thought, nuance, and complexity and have slipped into a sea of relativism.

Into the Nightmare

On Wednesday, January 20, exactly eight days, almost to the minute, after the catastrophic earthquake rocked Haiti, I boarded a plane at Bob Hope Airport in Burbank, California, bound for Dallas, Texas, where I joined a charter flight headed for Port-au-Prince with a team of doctors and nurses volunteering with CURE International from Lemoyne, Pennsylvania. We were told to pack very light to make room for more sorely needed medical supplies. It was a one-way flight; the return charter had not been arranged.

I was scared. Very scared. After a week of relative calm, the hunger and desperation within the people of Haiti had increasingly erupted into more widespread looting and violence. Hospitals were suddenly also treating gunshot wounds. A friend told me that a network camera crew was robbed and all their money and passports stolen. Each day, more American troops landed in Haiti in order to preserve order and help distribute food and water; the supplies were astonishingly still clogging the airport. Lots of aid was arriving in Port-au-Prince, but little was being distributed. Earlier in the week, helicopters began to drop pallets of water and ready-to-eat meals onto open fields. Often a mob of starving people rushed to the spot of the drop and fought over the food and water. And the airport was still a mess. A French helicopter pilot who flew me over the city in December for some aerial shots for the film sent me an e-mail saying the current situation at the airport was "absolutely insane." The night before this return trip, a plane chartered by Doctors Without Borders was diverted to Santo Domingo, thereby adding at least twenty-four hours to their journey. For so many of the injured, every additional minute without treatment decreased their chances of survival.

Yes . . . I was scared. But I had to go. Upon arrival in Haiti, the team of doctors and nurses would be transported to one of a few "safe" houses. These were homes not damaged by the earthquake and whose owners opened them up to those coming to help. All we were guaranteed was space on the floor to sleep and a limited supply of water and food.

At home on the morning of the trip, I did not want to come out of the shower. I stood there for perhaps ten minutes allowing the hot water to wash over me. It was calming and pleasant. I knew it would be my last hot shower for a long time. I thought about all the people in Haiti struggling with severe dehydration and how we take our precious sister water for granted. We cannot begin to fathom hauling heavy buckets of water from a common pump to our home. In Haiti, a person might consume or use less than two gallons a day. In the States, we use on average about 130 gallons each per day. We water lawns and wash cars without giving water a second thought. After the shower, I heard a report on CNN that a 6.1 aftershock had just hit Haiti. Yet, oddly enough, I was beginning to feel a sense of calmness, perhaps comforted by the knowledge that I was flying on the wings of prayers. I was deeply touched by the outpouring of pledges of prayer support I had received since I announced I was heading back to Haiti. In order for me to really work effectively I had to reach a still point within myself in order to capture with my camera the images that showed the profoundly moving and sympathetic faces of the stoic Haitians as they faced disaster with all the courage and dignity they could possibly muster. Only in stillness could I be truly attentive to the human moments that I hoped to photograph. For me, the camera becomes an instrument of prayer; and never was that more true than it would be on this trip.

Testing Grace

I had two beers on the flight to Dallas . . . a little treat to help me sleep. But there would be no sleeping. I really wasn't scared. Of course, I was concerned about how I would respond to all the widespread suffering I would witness . . . and the bodies in the streets. My time in Africa had already left me with a case of posttraumatic stress disorder, which was diagnosed when a severe panic attack resulted in a trip to the emergency room because it was feared that I had had a stroke. Haiti was one gigantic emergency room . . . without enough doctors or medicine. It felt sickening to pack Vaseline to put on my nose to lessen the stench of decaying bodies.

Could I deal with what I was going to see?

In the past, when people asked me how I film the agony on full display in my films, I responded by saying, "When God gives you a job to do, God also gives you the grace you need to do it." I believe that; but I knew that belief would be severely tested during my upcoming time in Haiti. Would I pass the test?

Turning a Passenger Jet into a Cargo Plane

The flight landed on time in Dallas, where I was met by a volunteer from a local church who drove me to a restaurant where the medical team arriving from all over the country would assemble and get to meet each other. Around eleven o'clock at night we were all driven in a caravan of cars to a private airport. We entered a huge hangar and were stunned to discover a sparkling white 737 commercial jet being loaded with medical supplies. I had envisioned some small plane, with room for just twenty-two people. But this was a big jet . . . and there was space for only twenty-two passengers because the rest of the plane was jammed with vital, much-needed medical supplies. We learned that it had taken almost the entire day to load the plane. The captain, copilot, and the two flight attendants could not have been any friendlier. With the last-minute loading of supplies, along with loading our luggage, a briefing from CURE International, and, believe it or not, a full security inspection of each of us, we did not push out of the hangar until shortly after three in the morning. En route to Haiti, some slept, some talked, some read. Breakfast was served about an hour before we landed. I was truly excited about returning to Port-au-Prince, but I was nervous about what I would encounter.

Smooth Landing

As we neared Haiti, I was hoping and praying we would be able to land and not be diverted to the Dominican Republic. We are all pretty exhausted already, and a ten-hour drive to Port-au-Prince would have been a bummer. Some members of the team did not learn they would be coming until early in the day on Wednesday, which meant they had a scant few hours to pack and make arrangements to be away for at least a week. We arrived over the island around 7:30 Thursday morning. We circled the airport for about an hour, as the tension over whether we would be able to land or not grew. But finally just before 8:30 a.m. we were cleared for landing. My hunch is that because our big jet contained so much medicine, including morphine, and medical supplies we were given a high priority for landing.

There was a rush of excitement as we walked down the stairs to the tarmac. It was a bright, sunny, warm Caribbean day. The noise and chaos at the airport was stupendous. Gigantic military cargo planes were coming and going at a dizzying pace. Helicopters were continuously flying overhead. At least thirty or forty helicopters were parked in a field on the other side of the single runway. The U.S. military presence was everywhere. Soldiers were moving supplies, unloading planes, and escorting elderly and injured Haitians to cargo planes for evacuation. I liked seeing an armed soldier pushing an old woman in a wheelchair across the tarmac to a cargo plane, stopping occasionally to bend down and tell her something, perhaps just a reassuring word. The small terminal building was jammed with people trying to get out of Haiti. Relief workers and Haitians all mixed together in a sea of confusion, all vying for the few available spaces on outgoing planes. It is hard to convey in words the intensity of the noise and constant movement at the airport. Off in the distance I could see mountains of off-loaded supplies waiting to be transported to the city. Also, the airport was surrounded by a maze of tents housing military personnel, media outlets, and field hospitals. It was organized chaos.

We did not have much of a chance to take in the extreme busyness at the airport and its air of excitement because we had to immediately begin the arduous task of unloading the medicine. Everyone pitched in and helped with the heavy lifting. It took a full two hours to get everything off the plane and onto two rickety old trucks. And then we were off . . . on a journey to the hospital and into the unknown. Most of us had a mixture of excitement and apprehension.

Clogged Streets

Most of the team rode in an old school bus. I was hoping to film as we drove, but shooting out the dirty window of the bus wouldn't work. I noticed Dr. Greg Bellig, an anesthesiologist from Sacramento, California, was going to be riding on the bed of a truck loaded with the supplies, just to make sure no one stole anything along the way. I asked him if I could join him. He helped me up and off we rode. I had a clear, unobstructed view. But it was bouncy ride and hard to hold on and film at the same time. Still, I managed a few good shots of the destruction along the route. But what caught our attention more than the collapsed buildings were the people standing or walking alongside the road. Many looked dazed and bewildered. Clearly some were still in a state of shock or still in the grips of grieving for lost family and friends. Others were desperate for help, begging us for anything. One woman pleaded for soap. Many touched their stomachs in a way that said they were hungry. We saw signs begging for food and water, and signs indicating the number of dead trapped inside a pile of rubble. For me, having seen the vibrancy of the city just weeks before, the deadly impact of the earthquake became more tangibly real and more heartbreakingly sad.

Into the O.R.

After a two-hour drive, our little caravan finally reached our destination, the Haitian Community Hospital, around 1:30 Thursday afternoon. Before the earthquake, even in traffic, the drive from the airport to the hospital would have taken no more than forty-five minutes. The last leg of the drive was up a hill along a road that dead-ended at the hospital. As we got closer to the hospital we began to see beds lining the road. Some beds were in makeshift tents, others out in the open, unprotected. As our truck drove slowly past the injured, I was stunned by the sight of so many people who clearly were seriously injured.

The hospital is located in the hilltop suburb of Pétionville. Medical volunteers from around the world camped out on the hospital rooftop and pulled fifteen-hour shifts, working tirelessly to meet the needs of the endless stream of patients, many with severe crush injuries. The basic plan already in place was simple: work to exhaustion, catch some sleep in tents on the hospital rooftop, and then work some more. And so it went, day after day, night after night, with volunteer teams coming and going. The hospital had several hundred patients and their families jamming hospital rooms, camped in halls, or living outside in tents. Running water was intermittent, creating huge sanitation problems. Electricity came from a diesel generator that sometimes faltered. Swatting mosquitoes, a team of plastic surgeons from the States set up a surgery suite in two rooms with ancient window-unit air conditioners and one rusty operating-room light.

Among the first doctors to arrive in Haiti after the earthquake was a thirteen-member team from New York; they ended up at the Haitian Community Hospital and were shocked to see thousands of injured Haitians lying on the floor inside the hospital or on the ground outside the hospital, some lying on boards, some on stretchers, some on mattresses. There were only two functioning operating rooms; the

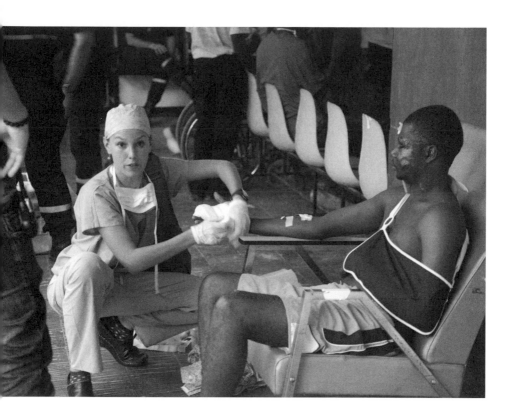

anesthesia machine did not work; there was no blood supply; and the labs were not functioning. Still, in an intense, exhausting three-day period they performed forty amputations and sixty limb-saving operations. But it was hard for them to adjust to the grim reality of so many amputations, because they were in the habit of saving legs. When the team had to leave, they needed a military escort to get them through the mob of people who did not want to see these skilled surgeons leave. But other teams of doctors would come, and keep coming. And after getting home, many doctors were so profoundly moved by the dire plight of the Haitians that they pledged to return.

The doctors and the nurses were quickly escorted to a room on the second floor where they dropped their bags and headed back downstairs to get to work. I dropped my bags, grabbed my video and still cameras, and followed along. My first interest was photographing the street outside the hospital. The word "overwhelming" is often overused, but in this case it simply does not convey what I saw. The combination of seeing such serious injuries, hearing so much moaning and crying, and smelling the stench of God only knows what pushed me to my limits of endurance. I did my best to take a few photographs, but I felt as if I were intruding on private moments of agony. I went back into the hospital and spent some time in the triage area, which occupied all of an indoor, open-air courtyard. You could see the bright sky above and the dark pain below. The screams of the children reverberated throughout the courtyard. I did what I had to do . . . film and photograph. And I listened and observed and tried to absorb it all. Everyone was busy tending to patients or rushing here and there for medical supplies. Doctors held up X-rays to the sunlight. Nurses soothed a frightened child or gave an adult an injection. Medics bandaged wounds. I watched . . . and prayed.

Eventually, I wandered the halls of the hospital, stealing glances in the rooms with hand-written signs indicating they were pre-op and post-op care. I did not lift either camera. I just walked . . . and prayed.

In time, I returned to the break room where our bags had been stored. I needed a little space to think about what I should be doing. The room had a supply of snacks and bottled water. As I was going through my camera bag, a doctor began to talk with me. I told him about my television history and my ministry, and he seemed genuinely interested in the films I had made for the San Damiano Foundation. Then he asked, "Have you seen the operating rooms?" "No," I answered. "You can tag along with me if you're interested in seeing them." Before I knew what was happening, I was being asked to put on a surgical gown and head covering, plus little booties to wear over my shoes. I was escorted into an operating room. And without flinching, I filmed two orthopedic surgeons operate on a woman, each doctor working on one of her legs. It was my baptism of fire; after this I would be able to film anything, and hopefully do so as coolly and professionally as the doctors had performed the double surgery. I'll skip the details of what they did, but, after the initial incision was made, it was very interesting. And they saved her legs. Later I was given a detailed explanation of what they did. It was kind of like making furniture, only with bleeding.

Floor Space

Before the trip, I was told that the team would be staying in a few safe houses. These were homes that had not been damaged by the earthquake, and the owners were poor people who would be happily opening their homes in gratitude for the doctors and nurses coming to help. All we were promised in these safe houses was space on the floor to sleep. Well, part of that plan was accurate. We did have space on the floor to sleep . . . but the floor was in the hospital. More specifically, it was in the luggage-laden break room. At night, virtually every inch of floor was occupied by luggage, supplies, or sleeping bags. Many of the volunteers elected to sleep on the roof, either in tents or on cots. The room was divided into two sections; besides the main large part of the room, there was a smaller room where water and snacks were kept. Off the smaller room was a bathroom with one toilet and one sink . . . for all of us. Amazingly, no one complained about the cramped quarters.

From Organized Chaos to Vast Destruction

My second day in Haiti was long and hard, and the day never offered me a chance to recover from the first day, with its protracted journey from the States and the shock of seeing so much destruction and suffering. I didn't get much sleep that first night. Doctors and nurses were in and out of the break room all night. A light was always on. Sleeping on the floor near the door to the bathroom wasn't a good idea. And one nurse snored like three truck drivers. In the morning, the line for the one toilet, for both men and women, was long. We stood around awaiting our chance to brush our teeth, passing the time eating Pop-Tarts; one wall was lined with boxes of them. Just moving around the room was tricky due to the clutter of suitcases and medical supplies. Down the hall from our little "home" there was a room with two additional toilets, as well as two showers. At one point, nurses and doctors, including surgeons, were lined up twelve deep waiting to take a shower. And just to add to the fun, there was a fairly strong aftershock that measured 6.0, big enough to get everyone's attention.

I got ready as quickly as I could and headed downstairs to the main part of the hospital. The triage area was already very intense, and so I decided to ease my way into the day by checking on the patients who had spent the night under the stars. I walked up and down the road outside the hospital and watched as the injured patients began another day of suffering and struggling. Family members helped them brush their teeth and gave them a little something to eat . . . if they had any food to eat. As I walked, people pointed to their stomachs or held out their empty hands saying they were hungry. I wished I could give them all something to eat. It was hard getting used to seeing so many people recovering from serious injuries lying on very old beds or on the ground. Imagine being in pain from a traumatic injury and sleeping outdoors at night. There were only a few portable toilets outside the hospital, and they were a considerable walk from most of the beds. The stench of urine permeated the air. I did not count them, but I would guess there were at least one hundred people outside the hospital, and at least a half dozen of them had one or more limbs amputated. Many patients had

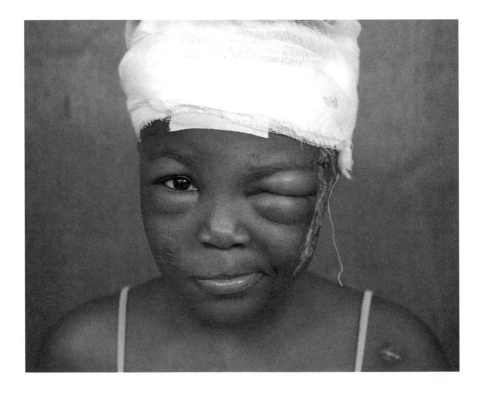

to choose between a limb or their life. I found it very difficult to film people in such desperate situations. Before lifting up the camera, I always spoke to the people first, expressing my sympathy in either words or a gesture (such as touching the left side of my chest over my heart), and asked for their permission to photograph them. As I walked back to the hospital entrance, I saw two men carrying a woman out of the hospital. She was seated on a simple chair; her lower left leg had been amputated. In post-earthquake Haiti, even a wheelchair is a luxury.

By nine in the morning, the hospital was already jammed with incoming wounded. As I walked around the triage area and the pre-op and post-op wards, I was deeply impressed by the courage and endless work of medical volunteers—doctors, nurses, physicians' assistants, and paramedics—from around the globe, as they attempted desperately in the worst circumstances to treat endless streams of patients, not always successfully. When they weren't working in the jury-rigged operating rooms and emergency rooms and makeshift wards out on sidewalks, I saw them fixing a door, sweeping the floor, and loading and unloading supplies. There was no medical hierarchy in this hospital, as everyone pitched in to do whatever needed to be done.

Driving around Hell

There was one doctor from Las Vegas on the team who had a certain lightness of being about him. He had a ready smile and a quick wit that delivered funny commentary on our common life of service. Plus he seemed to have endless little sweet, fun treats in his bag, which he happily tossed to the doctors and nurses, which always managed to bring a smile to their faces. His name is Dr. Mike Fishell, and he is an anesthesiologist. After doing a little filming in the hospital, I returned to the break room on the second floor for some water. In truth, I had already seen enough suffering and was not yet comfortable capturing it on film. I spotted Dr. Mike packing medical supplies into a suitcase and I heard him mention he would be delivering them to another hospital. I asked if I could tag along. Our destination was the Adventist Hospital, a seventy-bed facility with modern operating rooms. It was shaken by the earthquake but did not sustain any serious damage, and so it was overwhelmed with incoming wounded in the first few days of the disaster.

On our way to the hospital we asked the driver to take us on a short tour of the decimated downtown area around the Presidential Palace. Before reaching downtown, we stopped a few times so I could film the devastation. Outside a collapsed hotel, Dr. Mike confirmed that the stench heavy in the air was that of decaying flesh. We walked around the rubble of a college that was pancaked. We were told the bodies of at least fifty people were still inside. Most people in the vicinity were wearing some sort of mask or covering over their faces to ward off the noxious odor from the corpses. When we reached downtown Port-au-Prince we could not believe what we were seeing. The scope of the devastation was far beyond what the news had been able to communicate. We walked for three or four blocks in the area behind the palace, which was virtually completely leveled. Downed power lines and crushed cars made the streets almost impassable. We were stunned by the massive tent city that had sprung up in a large park near the palace. On the sidewalk that borders the park, I saw a teenage girl bathing her naked little brother. At one point, she paused, pulled down her shorts, squatted, and urinated. As she was relieving herself, the little boy turned toward the wall and also urinated. When she was finished, the girl casually stood up, pulled up her shorts, and resumed bathing the boy. It was a brief almost still moment in time that stood out in the swirling chaos and insane destruction, revealing a basic private human function forced to be performed in public. In Port-au-Prince everything is now public.

One week after the earthquake the United Nations estimated that about 700,000 people were sleeping outdoors at night, most of them concentrated in nearly 600 makeshift camps scattered across the shattered city. The displaced people used blankets, sheets, and curtains to form canopies, which provided protection from the sun but will be useless when it rains. And when the rains do come, what is already unbearable will be even more so . . . with the added possibility of epidemics from waterborne disease looming larger. The rainy season in Haiti begins in April; without tents for the homeless there will be another disaster.

As we headed out of the downtown area, we made one quick stop so I could film a crowd of people squeezing their way into an old bus that was headed out of Port-au-Prince. The roof of the bus was littered with everything that possibly could be carried. Huge numbers of people were fleeing Port-au-Prince and headed for the provinces. There was nothing left in the city for them, and life in the newly sprouted refugee camps was beyond intolerable. I photographed people literally trying to squeeze into the back door of the bus. Meanwhile, in the front of the bus, the driver was under the bus trying to fix a problem with the axle. It looked like a totally hopeless situation. People were pushing and shoving to get into a bus that seemed destined to break down long before it reached its destination.

During the remainder of our drive to the Adventist Hospital we continued to witness jaw-dropping destruction. One street was blocked by so much fallen debris that the driver had to turn around and find an alternate route to the hospital. The Adventist Hospital has far more property than the hospital where we were staying, and patients were being treated throughout the grounds. Because it is located closer to the center of the city, it has been inundated with enormous numbers of injured since the earthquake. The director of the hospital seemed overjoyed with the delivery of medicine Dr. Mike had brought. It was quickly determined that Mike's skills were more needed at Adventist Hospital than at the Haitian Community Hospital, and so he elected to stay there. I wanted to photograph the large numbers of people living in tents outside the hospital, but the driver had to get back to the Haitian Community Hospital, and so I had to go with him or risk being stuck far from all my camera equipment that was tucked safely in the break room at HCH.

A Life-and-Death Crisis

On the drive back, the driver let me jump out a few times to take photographs. After changing videotapes and batteries, I decided to hang out in the break room for a little while. I was hungry and figured this was a good time to try out one of the MREs (meals ready to eat), which are staples of the military diet in combat regions. I waited my turn for the microwave. I was told the meat-loaf MRE was pretty good. It was dreadful, but I was happy to eat it . . . and wished I could have served all the people in beds outside the hospital an MRE.

Just as I was finishing my meat loaf (and trying to figure out what kind of meat was in the loaf), a nurse came rushing into the room, saying there was an emergency in the recovery room and she needed some towels that had to be heated up. Someone told her where there was a supply of towels. Minutes later she returned with the towels and said she needed to wet them and then heat them in the microwave. She went into the bathroom, but there was virtually no water pressure, so she ran off to the other bathroom at the end of the hall, saying as she left to keep the microwave oven free because she would be right back. As she heated the wet towels she told a doctor that a teenage boy who had had both his legs amputated had taken a turn for the worse and was running a high fever. I was unable to follow the rest of the medical jargon regarding other post-operative concerns for the boy, but it was thought the best immedi-

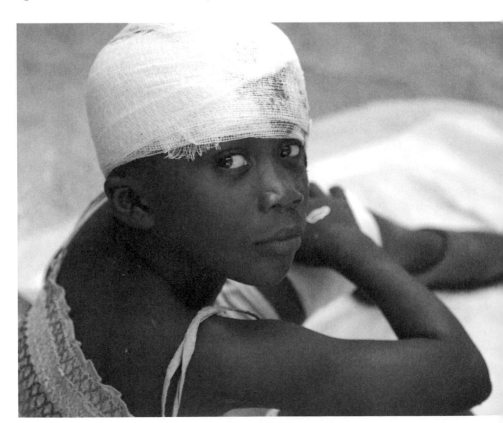

ate treatment would be to wrap the boy in warm towels. I asked the nurse if I could film her treating the boy. She paused for a second, and then said it would be OK. As she ran downstairs and through the long series of corridors to the recovery room, I had a hard time keeping up with her. Not only was she fast but she was very adept at weaving her way through the busy corridors lined with patients lying on the floor. As the distance between us grew greater, I wondered if this was worth the effort. I kept running.

As the nurse treated the boy, I could not help but hear a loud and increasingly urgent exchange between the doctors and nurses surrounding the bed of another patient. I decided to see what the cause of the commotion was. You did not need to be a doctor to quickly realize the medical staff was dealing with a life-and-death emergency. The patient was in cardiac arrest, and they were feverishly working to resuscitate her. Leading the effort was an anesthesiologist from the States but not part of the CURE team that traveled from Dallas. His name was Jack, and the night before we had a long conversation about the hospital. He even took me to the recovery room, where I filmed him talking about a woman patient who had lost both her legs and had developed a serious condition, and that despite his best efforts to combat it, he felt she would not make it through another day. As I filmed him, I could see how much he cared, and how frustrated he was that he could not do more.

And so as I stood a respectful distance away from the bed where the doctors and nurses were trying to resuscitate the woman, I felt a connection to Dr. Jack. We even exchanged a brief moment of eye contact. And so, I thought it was OK to lift up my camera and film the dramatic moment, which for me captured just how hard everyone was working to save as many lives as possible. I made sure I was not in anyone's way, and that my cinematic interest was in the doctors' valiant efforts, not the impending death of the woman. I worked with utmost sensitivity and sympathy, my heart breaking over the plight of not just this one woman, but all the injured I had seen, including the teenage boy in the next bed as the nurse tried to reduce his fever with towels heated in a microwave oven. All of Haiti was in a life-and-death crisis.

I must say it is extremely difficult for me to film the intense suffering I have seen around the world. I hate it. But it is truly what I feel called to do, so people can see the stark reality of chronic poverty . . . and perhaps do something to lessen the suffering. I was keenly aware at that moment that I was filming a nameless woman teetering on the precipice of eternity . . . where God knows her name and loves her and is waiting to embrace her in the fullness of divine love.

And then, without warning, one doctor working on the woman suddenly became enraged over my filming. He got right into my face and said, loudly and forcibly, to get out of the room. I can't recall his exact words, but in essence he said I was insensitive and disrespectful. He demanded to know who I was and what I was doing there. I do recall him saying, forcibly, "News crews don't belong in here." Someone came to my defense and said I was with the Dallas team and I had a right to be there. But rather than draw attention to myself or my intentions, I simply left the room as quickly as possible so everyone could concentrate on the woman.

As I walked back to the break room, I felt hurt. I wished I could just go home, just walk away from all the heartache and death. Even before this incident in the recovery room, I was already feeling useless and unneeded. Everyone else was saving lives. I was filming . . . and some of the medical staff and some of the injured did not appreciate my doing so. I questioned my reasons for being there. Was I helping the people of Haiti?

Filming poverty is different from filming a disaster. And in a case where the disaster is in an area of intense poverty the tension is dramatically increased. Filming the reality of the disaster in Haiti, where life-and-death situations are constant and where death, indeed, is too much part of the story, is essential in helping us understand the paramount importance of compassion, which has the capacity to not only comfort the hurting but also unite us in our common humanity.

When I reached the break room, my emotions and feelings of rejection still raw, I spotted a distinguished-looking black doctor seated on the ledge overlooking the courtyard triage area. I felt like talking with him, but did not want to intrude on his rare moment of stillness. He looked physically exhausted. But he asked me how I was doing, and I told him what had just happened in the emergency room and how badly I felt. He was from the nearby island of St. Thomas. He

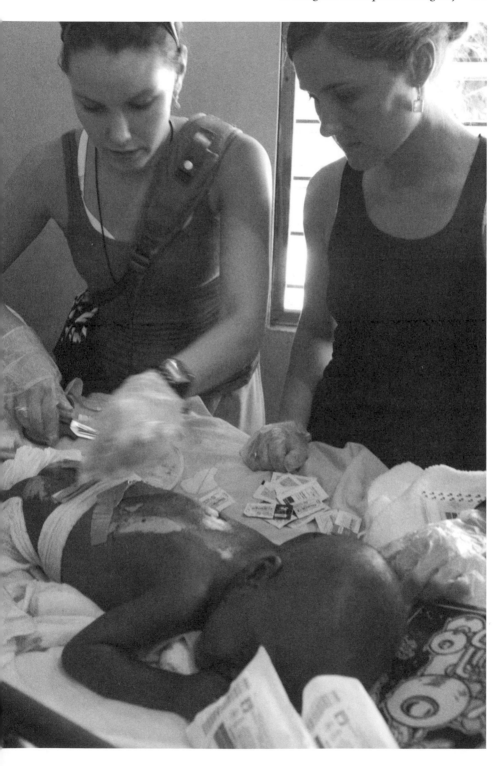

spoke briefly about the tension doctors have when they are on the verge of losing a patient. Then he said, "Let me tell you a story."

He had arrived in Port-au-Prince just days after the earthquake. A short time later he was joined by a colleague from St. Thomas whom he had asked to come help him. The doctor walked into the main entrance to the hospital and asked for directions to the operating rooms. But before an answer came, he was immediately pulled into the triage area where nurses were trying to resuscitate a young boy who was in septic shock. After working on the boy for a few minutes, the doctor decided to declare the boy dead. But others were urging him to continue to try to resuscitate him. The doctor said, "Even if we manage to revive him, there is nothing here to sustain him." After leaving the triage area, the newly arrived doctor saw his friend rushing into the operating room. He went to join him. The first surgery he did was to amputate the leg of a fifteen-month-old baby who had been trapped in rubble of his collapsed home. The mother had died beneath the rubble.

After finishing the story, the doctor looked at me and said, "And that was my friend's first hour in this hospital. He failed to revive a child and amputated the leg of an infant. Normal conventions don't apply in post-earthquake Haiti. Don't let being tossed out of the recovery room bother you."

That story and reassuring phone calls to Tom Roberts and a friend in Kentucky helped me quiet my feelings of uselessness. And the next day several of the medical personnel present when I was booted out of the recovery room said that they were confident I was there not to sensationalize the moment, but to record as many aspects of the emergency as possible. Someone also told me that the offended doctor later was convinced of the worth of my efforts. I also learned that the woman being resuscitated and the teenage boy with the high fever both died.

It was impossible to keep count of the numbers of children and adults I saw in and around the hospital with missing limbs, amputations that were necessary because it had taken so long for patients to reach the hospital that crushed limbs had become gangrenous and irreparable. Yet amid it all, it was amazing to see the outpouring of compassion. To me, that was the real beauty within this bleak world of the aftermath of the earthquake. Nobody wanted to be pampered, nobody was pulling a superior attitude. They were just working. They were living on power bars and Gatorade that they brought in with them as they gave themselves fully and without reservation to the poor of Haiti. They were living the gospel . . . and it was truly magnificent to behold.

Trapped

As I was preparing to go to sleep on Friday night, a nurse suggested that instead of sleeping on the floor I should go up on the roof where I could find a cot that I could bring back to the break room. It was a good idea. The cot was better than the floor, but not much better. On Saturday morning, I spotted another chance to get out of the hospital and spend time on the streets. Two young nurses from Chicago were going to go to a private home close to the center of the city, where they would set up a one-day field clinic to treat the less seriously injured. When we arrived, there was already a line of people waiting. Most of the injuries were cuts, some of which had not been treated, and others were cuts that had been treated but the bandages had not been changed for days.

After filming for a few hours, I met a guy from the neighborhood who was acting as a translator. His name was Reginald. As we talked, I mentioned my desire to see more of the destruction near center city. He said he would see if he could borrow a car and take me on a tour of some very hard-hit areas that few outsiders had seen. He was back within thirty minutes. As we drove, he was happy to stop wherever I wished to photograph. At one location, we spotted the skeletal remains of a person partially trapped by a collapsed hotel. From the visual evidence, it seemed that as the hotel collapsed during the earthquake, it snapped some electrical wires and ignited a small fire. The victim was trapped from the waist down under the collapsed structure . . . and was burned to death. The skeletal remains of the victim remained unmoved for eleven days. Who knows how many people were trapped inside . . . the stench was sickening.

As we continued our drive, I made many stops to film the devastation. As Reginald waited in the car, I often ventured more than a block away from him. I never felt threatened or in danger from any of the people, many of whom were sifting through the rubble looking for anything they could salvage. I saw no evidence of the widespread violence and looting that the news had reported. I walked unescorted around downtown with cameras worth over $5,000 and never encountered a hint of trouble. People were calm and courteous. I became concerned only once. We had parked in an area where the destruction seemed worse than anything we had seen. The street was impassable. The stench of death was so overpowering I had to wear an air filter over my mouth and nose. When we returned to the car, it would not start. There were a lot of young people around and they were arguing over something. I worried that we would have to walk a long distance if the car did not start and we would be totally unprotected the entire time. But it did start. However, it kept stalling out. Reginald had a hunch the gas station had diluted the gas with water in order to increase its profits and minimize the impact of the gas shortage.

When we arrived back at the clinic, I tried to give Reginald some money. He refused to accept it. I said, "Please, take it, if only to replace the gas you used driving me around." Again he refused. He said that I had come to Haiti during his nation's moment of true need and he could not accept money from someone trying to help the people of Haiti. Reginald's unwillingness to accept the money gives a little hint of the noble character of most Haitians, even during the midst of a severe crisis.

The nurses closed the clinic in the early afternoon, and we returned to the hospital. On the drive back, one nurse fell sound asleep, exhausted from the nonstop work. As soon as we arrived at the hospital, the nurses put in a full eight-hour shift, working until near midnight.

Living the Gospel

The first three days in Haiti left little time for reflection and virtually no time to put any thoughts down on paper. Each day was crammed with images of destruction, suffering, and death. But I also witnessed extraordinary courage and faith within the suffering

Haitian people. They live in the grace of acceptance and hope. Haitians have a fierce resilience, and in the wake of the earthquake they have nothing left but their beautiful humanity and gracious dignity. The amazing outpouring of compassion and help from all over the world truly astounded me and showed me just how much gentle, unseen goodness there is in the world and within people.

On Saturday night, January 23, at the end of our third day, I was exhausted and beginning to feel the strain of living in such cramped quarters. Suddenly, much to my amazement, I was gifted with a little space and silence. I was graced to be standing in the right place when a young man offered two doctors a chance to spend the night at his parents' home just down the road from the hospital. He said he had space and, more important, a hot shower. He knew about my filming and asked if I wanted to come also. I said it would be better for another doctor to have a good night's sleep and hot shower. He said he was leaving right then and all the doctors were busy so I might as well escape the hospital. I grabbed my bags and happily left the crowded break room that had been my home.

After two nights of sleeping in a room at the hospital, in a cluttered space shared by a dozen doctors and nurses sleeping on the floor surrounded by luggage and boxes of medical supplies, with people coming and going all night long, I unexpectedly found myself in a beautiful private home safely tucked away behind a wall and a secured gate. There was stillness and room to unpack all my camera gear. I had a bed, a hot shower, and an excellent home-cooked meal. I never enjoyed a glass of wine so much in my life.

There was so much to take in. The endless misery and suffering at the hospital. Three patients died on Saturday. The utter devastation of downtown. The haunting image of the charred skeletal remains of a person who died at the moment of the earthquake. The tent cities that occupy every large, open air space, from parks to soccer fields, throughout the city. Tens upon tens of thousands of people desperate for food and water.

As I lay in bed, the horror of all I had seen these past few days randomly floated across my mind. All the amputees. The crumbled buildings. The constant pleas for help. The kids and the adults bathing in the streets, naked. I could not get used to seeing seriously injured people lying on old hospital beds or on the ground outside the hospital. Their families made little shelters out of what they had. An old sheet served as a canopy to keep the blazing sun off the injured family member. Why was I in such a pleasant and safe space? What I had was really rather basic, yet it was far, far beyond what the millions of chronically poor of Haiti will ever experience. I felt a pang of guilt, felt unworthy to have such precious space. Yet, I really needed it because I felt I was truly hitting an emotional wall and doubted I could have lasted much longer in the hospital with its nonstop agony and noise.

As I was falling asleep I tried to imagine myself in the position of a patient sleeping on the ground outside the hospital. I could not. I've deceived myself into thinking I live simply, that I don't require much to get through each day. But my lifestyle is far from simple, my perceived needs far from modest.

So many people have so many ideas of what to do in Haiti, how to recover, regroup, and rebuild. The mother at the home where I am staying talked at dinner last night about the overcrowding in Port-au-Prince that existed before the earthquake. The poor poured into the capital because there were no services or jobs in the provinces. When Aristide was toppled, the factories closed and the jobs disappeared. But the poor kept coming. And the hillside shanty towns and the slums kept expanding. The mother said the answer is not to simply rebuild Port-au-Prince. The relief aid, she insisted, must be spread across the provinces. Hospitals, schools, and housing must be built outside of Port-au-Prince. If houses are built in Port-au-Prince, word will spread like wildfire and there will be a huge influx of the poor back into Port-au-Prince and it will overwhelm the effort to rebuild. During the past week, there has been a mass exodus of biblical proportions. People are leaving Port-au-Prince, fleeing the chaos, disease, and lack of food and water.

On Sunday morning I decided not to rush out with the two doctors staying at the home. I sat in my little kitchen and rearranged and organized all my stuff. I realized I left the battery charger at the hospital in my haste to escape. I scribbled some random thoughts in my journal . . . and prayed for some insight into what I should be doing with what I am seeing.

No great revelations came. But one phrase came to mind and stayed: live the gospel. I wondered if the gospel has really penetrated into the core of my being. I don't think so.

Life and Death

After a good night's sleep and a slower, more reflective pace in the morning, I was ready to head up to the hospital. I was happy to catch a ride with a family member who was driving up the hill. As I got out of the car, a team from Mississippi was bringing the remains of a deceased person to an area adjacent to some garbage dumpsters. The corpse was in a giant trash bag. The deceased was placed next to two other corpses. The team headed back to the hospital to get the remains of a fourth person. I walked closer to the bags. Flies were buzzing around them and the stench was truly repugnant. I paused, bowed my head, and said a silent prayer for the souls of the departed.

Later I talked with one of the team members charged with the unpleasant task of removing the dead from the hospital. He was visibly upset at the job he had to perform. He lamented that there was no way to notify the family so they could have a moment to see the deceased, say goodbye, and offer a prayer. Right after one corpse had been removed from the hospital, a relative showed up and became hysterical when they were told that they could not see their loved one one last time. The removal team did not want to show the family member where the body was because they felt that the undignified setting would be even more upsetting. Can you imagine being escorted to a sealed rubbish bag surrounded by flies lying not far from some trash to offer a farewell to someone you loved?

These small moments of life and death helped me better understand the disaster. I can't process 100,000 dead. But when I see the agony of a guy whose charred skeletal remains were trapped under a collapsed building and the loneliness of a dead patient stuffed into a plastic bag and left out in the sun, it becomes personal and real. Who were those people? What were their dreams?

I spent all day Sunday inside the hospital. I filmed one medical procedure that deeply disturbed me. It was performed in the open-air, inner courtyard that served as the triage area. Korean doctors were changing the bandages of a woman who had recently had her left leg amputated from just below the knee.

I filmed it, but I am not sure I can watch it. Before they began, I went up to the woman and put my hand on her shoulder and asked her permission to film the doctors at work. She said yes. I told her I was sorry for her injury. I stood well behind the doctors, as I switched back and forth between my still camera and my hi-def video camera. The overweight woman was perhaps in her late forties. She did not seem to be in any physical pain, but she did appear to be somewhat dazed and distant, either still in shock or perhaps heavily medicated. I am not sure exactly what happened, whether the wound from the amputation accidentally opened or the process of cleaning the wound necessitated the wound be opened. Either way, the unexpected sight of blood pouring out from the exposed end of her amputated leg stunned and disturbed me. One doctor held her hand, as two other doctors worked on cleaning and treating the wound. It was painful to watch. At one point, I put the cameras down and stood next to the woman and tried to comfort her as best as I could. To add to the drama of it all, there was a little girl about seven years old, seated on the floor next to the gurney where the doctors were treating the woman. The girl was heavily bandaged . . . and crying. Her tearful eyes had a truly frightened look to them. Between the girl's loud crying and the blood from the amputated leg, I felt as if I were in the midst of a cruel nightmare. And I think the medical people working on other injured people in the area also seemed horrified by the intensity and severity of the situation.

After filming the woman, I went to the roof and called Tom Roberts and my sister . . . and I cried. It was all too much. Their gentle and wise words helped me move to a state of peace where I could continue to work. I decided to spend a little time in the post-op area. I wanted to document the constant movement and noise. Some patients were outside the rooms, lying on beds that lined the walls of the large corridor. Some patients were on the floor. I had tucked myself alongside the nurse's station, so as not to block the busy flow of traffic while unobtrusively capturing the sense of urgency that filled the air. Near the end of the corridor, a nurse and a group of people were surrounding the bed of a patient. I walked near them to see what

was happening. The nurse turned, looked at me, and in an irritating tone snapped at me, saying that the patient was dying and I had no right to be intruding on this sensitive moment. In truth, I was not intruding. I was simply looking, not filming, and I was doing so from a respectful distance. This nurse had seen me working before, and for some reason the presence of the camera irritated her. And I think her irritation stemmed from the insensitivity in which a foreign camera crew who had been at the hospital earlier in the day went about their business. They were on the prowl for the most dramatic images they could find with little regard for the medical personnel or the patients. Once again, it was not pleasant to be snapped at, but I simply had to walk away and chalk up the nurse's surly attitude to her having to deal with a very stressful situation.

Later that afternoon, an amputated leg wrapped in plastic was placed next to the four body bags. On Monday someone made the gruesome discovery that a dog had torn through the plastic bag and gnawed away the lower leg of one of the corpses. What was left of the leg was found in the nearby woods. The hospital had made many calls to the city asking them to remove the bodies, but despite promises to do so no one ever showed up. So, in the face of the powerful smell and the vulnerability to wild dogs, the corpses were loaded onto a pickup truck on Monday evening and driven to the cemetery and placed outside the entrance.

Alone and Useless

I was so very happy to leave the hospital early Sunday evening and return to the silent tranquility of my room at Joelle and Pierre's home. I was still upset at the nurse snapping at me, and still horrified by the changing of the amputee's wound. I felt useless and unnecessary. Moreover, I felt intensely alone. The doctors and nurses are forming bonds. The many medical volunteers are part of a team. I am an outsider . . . with a camera. There are a few people that I've connected with on some simple level, but it does not go beyond knowing each other's names and saying hello as we pass in the halls. There is really no time to just talk . . . the work is relentless. I got through the weekend only because I was able to call Tom Roberts and my sister . . . and

pour my heart out to them, often crying as I spoke. They reassured me of the merit of what I was doing.

Everything Is Dead

Among the medical volunteers at the hospital were a bunch of Haitian medical students studying in the Dominican Republic. They came back to Haiti along with a Haitian doctor from the school to pitch in and help as best they could. For the most part, they worked in an area outside the hospital where they treated less serious injuries, but mostly changed bandages and performed other simple medical procedures, such as removing sutures, under the careful eye of the doctor. But on Monday morning I heard they were leaving the hospital to set up a one-day clinic at a refugee camp in a very poor neighborhood. I asked if I could tag along, and fortunately there was just enough space for me . . . as long as I was willing to have a petite female student sit on my lap during the drive. Oh, the sacrifices I am willing to make.

The crowded camp consisted of a small space between two buildings. Every inch of the ground was covered with blankets and makeshift tents. The population seemed to be mostly families, with lots of kids and older people. At the back of the camp, perhaps about 150 feet from the street, was an enclosed area where the medical students set up their field clinic. A line quickly formed. Most of the people seeking treatment had minor injuries or needed wounds cleaned. I filmed the camp and the clinic for a little while, but I soon became restless and eager to explore the surrounding neighborhood.

About two blocks from the camp was the base of a hillside shantytown where virtually all the poorly constructed concrete buildings had collapsed. I decided to walk up an alley that seemed somewhat clear of rubble. As I huffed and puffed my way up the hill it was hard to comprehend the level of destruction. Again, the stench of decaying bodies trapped in the rubble was overwhelming. I had to wear my mask over my mouth and nose, which made breathing during my slow uphill climb more difficult. I encountered many people walking up and down the hillside. I gave each one a gesture of sympathy. I encountered no trouble or hostility from anyone. I quickly grew weary of the uphill climb, made worse by all the camera equipment I was carrying, and so I decided to head back down.

As I neared the base of the hillside, I spotted the doctor who was accompanying the medical students. He was concerned by my absence and had come looking for me. We returned to the camp, and once the situation there seemed to be under control, the doctor asked if I still wished to explore the neighborhood. I said yes, and he said he would be happy to accompany me and act as a translator. He also indicated he wanted to see the damage for himself. As we approached the hillside, a young man came up to us and told us about all the dead people still buried in the rubble. He said it would be an honor to escort us to the top of the hill. And so the sad climb began. We paused often, as the young man told us about the families who had lived in each home. Many people had returned to try to salvage whatever they could of their humble possessions. They were walking down the narrow alleys carrying furniture and other household items. The job was made more difficult because of all the rubble they had to climb over or navigate around. The doctor, who gra-

ciously offered to carry my bag, often had to lend a hand to help me climb over a treacherous stretch of the climb. He also was pressed into action as a cameraman when I felt the need to make a comment on camera.

About halfway up the hill, our guide stopped to point out a charred spot on the ground. He told us how the residents were forced to burn the remains of their loved ones in order to prevent the spread of disease. In front of one collapsed home, a survivor looked right into my eyes and said, "Everything is dead."

Crucified with Christ

Early Tuesday morning (January 27), Dr. Greg Bellig and I managed to procure a van and a driver, and we headed out for what would be a five-hour drive around Port-au-Prince.

Driving through the ruined city, we could see the devastation everywhere we looked. Countless Haitians crammed every open public space where they camped beneath sheets and cardboard. Signs in multiple languages pleaded for food and water. The tropical air was hazy with concrete dust and reeked of excrement and death. Few building remnants had spray-painted Xs, indicating that they had been searched for survivors and bodies. One pile of rubble contained this heart-wrenching, spray-painted message: "Lots of dead people inside." The United Nations called it the worst disaster in the organization's sixty-year history. Our drive left us with no doubt about that claim.

As we headed out from the hospital, I was talking to Dr. Greg about Cité Soleil, and the driver thought I was asking to be taken there. The intensity level at the slum was extremely high. The center island that divides the main road that passes along the outskirts of Cité Soleil was jammed with make-shift tents. I told Greg that the area is dangerous and known for its brutal violence. I said we could get out of the van briefly to do some filming, but we would not leave the main road or venture too far from the van. Of course, we did wander farther from the van than we should have. All of a sudden, a caravan of large white trucks thundered down the road. They contained food. As the trucks rolled past us, we became engulfed in a wave of people run-

ning after the trucks. The trucks stopped a few hundred yards down the road and were instantly surrounded by a mass of hungry people desperate for food. We weaved our way through the onrushing crowd back to the van. The area seemed like a tinderbox ready to explode. We left immediately and headed for downtown.

Port-au-Prince may be surrounded by stunning natural beauty, but the architectural landscape of the city is truly ugly. There are two exceptions: the Cathedral of Notre Dame and the Presidential Palace, both located near each other in downtown. These landmark structures were truly elegant, looming presences that dwarfed the surrounding buildings in both size and splendor. Neither survived the earthquake, and their collapse came to symbolize the scope of devastation the people of Haiti had to face. In December I circled both buildings in a helicopter, which is the best way to capture their monumental grandeur on film. After we left Cité Soleil, I asked the driver to take us to the cathedral so I could photograph what I considered to be an icon of the tragedy that had befallen Haiti.

Of course, the irreplaceable loss of such a magnificent building is tremendous, but the ruins of this one church building also symbolize the severity of the damage to the church itself. After decades of unstable governance, scant infrastructure, and state-led institutions that barely functioned, it is the church that has taken up the slack and given Haitians some sliver of normalcy, opportunity, and hope. The church, including Catholics, Episcopalians, and Evangelicals, is the backbone of the educational and health care systems. The church cares for the orphans and the elderly. The church is at the forefront of preserving the dwindling environmental resources and protecting the rights of migrant workers who cross into the Dominican Republic in search of jobs.

It will take decades for the Catholic Church alone to recover from the disaster. More than one hundred priests and nuns are missing or dead. Ten seminarians riding on a bus after attending a conference were killed when a building fell on the vehicle. The National Major Seminary of Notre Dame of Haiti, the only major Catholic seminary in Haiti, was destroyed. The school's philosophy department lost eight of its ninety-seven seminarians; and more than a month after the earthquake they were still digging through the ruins of the theology department, but it was estimated that twenty seminarians were killed. One small example of the impact the earthquake has had on the church's work on behalf of the poor is to note that the Salesians ran eleven schools in Port-au-Prince and more than half of them have been destroyed. And it is almost certain that that scenario can be repeated over and over again among all the religious orders working in the city. I know the home of three Franciscan priests was destroyed.

Dr. Greg expressed a desire to see the toppled Presidential Palace, which was not very far from the cathedral. It was difficult to film the palace because of the fence that rings the property, which is the size of a least four square blocks. Seeing as I was wearing an ABC News hat which my friend gave me, I thought we could try to bluff our way into the compound for a little bit of unobstructive filming. The entire back of the complex consisted of the government's administrative buildings, virtually all of which were totally destroyed. We entered the property and were immediately stopped by armed guards. We told them we simply wanted one quick shot of the exterior of the front of the presidential palace. After our request

worked its way up the chain of command, it was eventually denied. We parked the car on the street behind the palace and set off on a five-block walking tour of the destruction in the cluttered area near the palace. The devastation was beyond comprehension, the stench of death still permeating the air.

After we returned to the van, we circled the block to the front of the palace. Along the way we passed a line of thousands of people patiently waiting for some kind of aid. It was a ridiculously long line, at least six people wide. There was no panic, no pushing or shoving . . . just an orderly line: waiting for who knows what.

As we headed home, we drove past Sacré Coeur (Sacred Heart) Church. I told Greg I had to stop, because I had been in the church in December. I saw a way into the church, which was totally destroyed. As I walked into the ruins, Greg said, "This is crazy." I said, "It's actually beyond crazy, but I'm going in." Without missing a beat, Greg said, "I'm right behind you." The walls were almost all gone, but somehow most of the ceiling had not fallen. The pews were covered with dust. We saw a cell phone on one pew, left behind as the owner rushed out of the crumbling church. A New Testament was on the floor near the tabernacle. I photographed the church and we left. Nearby, there is a grotto containing a statue of Our Blessed Mother. I remember sitting in front of it in December, as a few women prayed the rosary. Even more people were there today, still praying the rosary, perhaps more fervently so. Because of my cameras, they seemed a little bit annoyed by my presence. So I took my rosary out of my pocket and held it up, and, almost in unison, they all held their rosaries up and smiled. It was a sweet moment of solidarity.

Across the street from the church were the totally collapsed remains of the parish grammar school. As Greg and I walked though rubble, we saw many items that make a huge tragedy startlingly personal: notebooks, workbooks, school bags, papers. We could see into one classroom that had not collapsed and the sight of all the small desks facing the blackboard sent a chill down my spine. And then Greg noticed a decaying foot sticking out of the rubble. Based on the size of the foot, Greg said it was a child. We could see the cuff of a pair of pants and so we assumed it was a boy. The stench was sickening. We wondered how many other children were also buried in the rubble. You can get lost in the huge numbers of estimated dead, you can become numb, and then something happens like finding the boy that reminds you that the numbers are individuals. It brought things down to a personal level. One minute, he was studying, and then next moment he was buried under tons of concrete. Before leaving, we paused near the remains of the little boy and said a prayer.

Before returning to Haiti, I saw a TV news report in which the correspondent was standing in front of the destroyed church. I think he chose the spot because in front of the church there was a large crucifix with a life-sized replication of the dying body of Christ, his hands and feet nailed to the cross. I'm sure the news team felt it was a powerful image, the cross standing and the church collapsed in a single frame. However, it is also a powerful symbol of the crucified Haitian people who wait with hope for their resurrection.

The cross reminds us of Good Friday, brings us to the Hill of Calvary, the lonesome, disturbing place of suffering and pain, which became the intersection of hatred and love as the darkness of Good Friday yielded to the glorious light of Easter. The people of Haiti are experiencing their own Calvary, a bleak and empty place where the future is truly uncertain. We must reach out to them in their endless heart of loss and gently walk with them in our mutual vulnerability to the transformed reality of Easter.

After taking photographs of the cross, Dr. Greg and I headed up the mountain to the hospital.

Playing in the Ruins

Perhaps this is a good spot to offer a brief geographical note. Port-au-Prince's downtown is near sea level. It is the commercial and political center of the city. But as you leave downtown, heading away from the waterfront, the city gradually climbs up the slopes of the surrounding mountains. As you get higher, the city merges into Pétionville. I stayed in a hotel in Pétionville during my December visit. At first, Pétionville seemed virtually indistinguishable from Port-au-Prince. But I slowly saw that there were significant differences. Pétionville is where many of the minuscule upper class live and shop because it is farthest from the most densely populated,

poorest slums in the heart of Port-au-Prince. Two blocks from the hotel there is a restaurant that many consider to be the best in Haiti. But poverty is still present. The first place we filmed in December was a slum within walking distance of the hotel. It was an older, more established slum. The simple, concrete homes were more substantial than the tin shacks of Cité Soleil. People were packed into this hillside slum. The haphazardly built homes lined a maze of small alleys, far too small for cars. There was a constant flow of foot traffic in the steep and poorly paved alleys; people carried everything they needed, from food and water to furniture, into the slum. Life in this more upscale slum was hard, but far better than life in Cité Soleil. Across the street from the hotel was a large park where people could sit in the shade on benches. The road circling the park was lined with vendors selling flowers, art, and food. After the earthquake the park was crammed with tents, which I assume were occupied by the poor from the nearby hillside slum whose homes most surely had to have been severely damaged; and the hotel became the home of Anderson Cooper of CNN News.

As we drove back up the main road to Pétionville we could see a massive hillside slum on the other side of a canyon. In December, driving up the same road on our way to the hotel, we pulled off the road to film that slum from a distance. From that vantage point you could dramatically see the size of the slum and how packed together the homes were. I was told residents of the slum had to walk up and down the steep hill every day for everything they needed. There was no running water or electricity in the slum. As we drove today, I was shocked by what I saw. The vast majority of the homes had collapsed. Even from a distance, we could see people moving about the hillside, sifting through the mountain of rubble. It was clear that many people were still living there. I could see children playing in the ruins. I can't even imagine how many people from this hillside died in the earthquake; the exact number will never be known. No one is tending to the people who survived . . . they are on their own, as they were before the earthquake. For them the struggle continues, only it is far more intense now.

Much of Pétionville survived the quake because most of the buildings in the area were better built. Still, there were many poorer structures that had collapsed. After three fairly long driving tours of the city covering a wide sampling of neighborhoods, the sheer scope of the damage to the buildings forces me to try to imagine how to even begin to rebuild Port-au-Prince. Before any rebuilding can begin, the massive job of cleaning up must be faced. Debris removal will be a monumental job. There are millions upon millions of tons of rubble to be picked up and taken somewhere. But where? The logistics of moving so much shattered concrete and the crushed contents of the buildings is mind-boggling. Perhaps it all gets dumped into the sea. Just transporting the rubble over bad roads will be a significant challenge. It is a huge job in terms of technology, equipment, and money. Recovery and rebuilding is at minimum a twenty-five-year-long job. Most Haitians will never see the job completed. Many kids will grow up in a city of rubble.

Lost in Translation

So many people from so many different nations trying to communicate with the local population that speaks mostly Creole, some French, and a little English often presented many different translation challenges. One day I was walking down the corridor and I overheard a snippet of a conversation between one of the medical staff from America and a local translator . . . and it was more than enough to make me smile, even though translation problems could have fatal effects. A paramedic from Mississippi was asking the volunteer translator to tell a patient that he was "fixin' to discharge her." Try understanding that bit of Southern slang and expressing it in Creole.

I heard a doctor tell the translator to ask the patient when the last time her bandage had been replaced. The answer that came back: "Twenty years." Miscommunication was a real and potentially serious problem.

Tiffany and Yveline

This is the story of a bright, young nurse from Chicago and a little girl from Haiti who was pulled from the rubble of her home after being buried for three days. Before January 12, their worlds could not have been further apart. But now their hearts are forever connected. Amid the endless heartache that is Haiti, it is often the small, gentle connections that make the suffering bearable, that bring light to the darkness.

There was a young nurse on the team whose sparkle and empathy caught my attention. Her name is Tiffany Cupp, and she is twenty-eight years old. She seemed very mature and confident for her age. At the hospital in Haiti she worked mostly in the incoming triage area. She treated every patient with the utmost respect and dignity. Just watching her interact with the people, especially the children, I could sense her genuine compassion and concern. And she seemed tireless, always rushing about doing something, helping someone. She dove right into each situation, taking charge and handling each crisis as it arose. Tiffany is a registered nurse at University of Chicago Comer Children's Hospital as well as Children's Memorial Hospital. She was shocked by the first pictures out of Haiti after the earthquake, and her first impulse was a desire to help. On the Friday after the earthquake a nurse at work asked, "So, what do you think about going to Haiti as a relief member?" The instantaneous answer was, "Yes."

And so Tiffany spent the weekend surfing the web searching for organizations who were putting together medical teams to help the injured in Haiti. She was determined to find a spot on a plane bound for Port-au-Prince. The church she attends provided the connection she needed. On the Park Community Church's website there was a notice that CURE International was looking for nurses to join a team of surgeons that would be going to Haiti. She hounded CURE until they finally called her the following Tuesday at 3:30 p.m. and invited her to be part of the team leaving from Texas the next day. She had exactly twenty-four hours before catching a plane from Chicago to Dallas . . . and the 3:00 a.m. flight to Port-au-Prince.

On the morning of January 12, Yveline was an ordinary eight-year-old girl who loved playing with her family and friends. But her future was somewhat bleak before her world collapsed around her. Just days before the earthquake Yveline (pronounced Eveline) was diagnosed with type 1 diabetes. This particular type of diabetes requires strict management of the glucose level in her blood. Too much or too little glucose can be deadly. The condition would be nearly impossible to manage in a place like Haiti where there was no access to the proper medications and medical devices, especially for the poor. But diabetes would soon be the least of little Yveline's problems.

At 4:53 in the afternoon of January 12, Yveline and her family were at home when the 7.0 earthquake rumbled beneath their house. Theirs was one of at least 1.5 million homes destroyed within seconds. Following the sheer terror of those dreadful moments of shaking and the house collapsing, Yveline and her family were trapped in the rubble without any way to escape. This little angel of a girl watched as both her mother and father took their last breath and died. Not only was Yveline trapped but she was now alone lying motionless next to her dead parents. It is impossible to imagine her ordeal and the bravery she needed to muster in order to survive. Yveline was trapped under the rubble for three days, during which time her parents' corpses must have begun to decompose, before she was rescued. Her removal from the rubble made the news all around the world, and she became a little ray of hope in the bleak landscape of destruction and despair.

When she returned home after six intense days of caring for the injured, Tiffany posted a story on her blog about her relationship with Yveline. She wrote: "I remember Yveline sitting in a chair motionless with a severely injured right arm and wounds around her face—yet she was smiling at me when I approached her. It took me a while to learn the story of Yveline because she is a very shy young girl. She told me via an interpreter that she remembered her house falling and she was 'very sad because she knew her mom and dad died, but then after it became light again she was very sad again because she was so hungry.'"

During the collapse of her home, Yveline suffered a severe crush injury to her right arm that will most likely render it nonfunctional for the rest of her life. Still she is able to smile. Tiffany writes: "Yveline is by far the most extraordinary young person I have ever met. Not one day went by that she was not smiling or running around happy as can be." Tiffany believes Christ spared her so she could be a model of strength and courage to everyone she meets. "I sat and watched her as she played with a doll given to her by another relief team member from Sweden, as she brushed her doll's hair and put clothes on her doll. She was able to find a way to hold the doll between her legs while she used her left arm to brush her hair. I sat and thought to myself, 'I wonder what I would be like if I lost functionality of one arm, would I be able to function as well as she does?'"

As the week progressed Yveline was placed on the surgical schedule due to complications in her right arm, a complication called compartment syndrome due to her crush injury. This particular complication is repaired by a procedure called a fasciotomy, where the fascia in her arm is cut to relieve tension or pressure that could impair circulation of the affected extremity, thus causing the extremity to become dead. Following the procedure Yveline was suffering from extreme pain and refused to eat, drink, or talk to anyone. A nurse from Sweden found Tiffany and told her that Yveline was in extreme pain and began crying her name aloud.

Tiffany picks up the story on her blog: "After hearing this I raced to her room to find her lying on the ground (her bed) with tears streaming down her little face. Her aunt and grandmother were both at her bedside, however her aunt revealed that Yveline said, 'Tiffany makes my pain go away, where is she?' My heart melted knowing that my stay in Port-Au-Prince Haiti would soon come to an end however her suffering would remain forever. After knowing this I sat beside Yveline and rubbed her back while she held one of my hands tightly to her heart. She soon drifted into a slumber only to be woken every 2 hours in order to receive her needed medications and frequent assessments of her affected arm. The next morning Yveline woke with her brilliant smile sparkling asking if I would sit and play with her doll 'Tiffany'. I again sat beside her mesmerized at her ability to cope with everything she had endured in the past 13 days. My final day in Haiti was extremely emotional knowing I would be leaving, not only Yveline but everyone else the Lord put in my path. My days were extremely long, but each day ended with the beautiful thought of my little Haitian angel . . . Yveline."

This is only one story out of the more than two million people who were affected by this earthquake. Yveline is among many who require our thoughts, prayers, and support. Tiffany is worried that Yveline's condition may deteriorate without our continued financial and spiritual support. She also worries what will happen when her eighty-eight-year-old grandmother is no longer around . . . the grandmother is Yveline's only living relative. Sadly, Yveline's situation is now common: it is estimated that as many as 380,000 children may have lost one or both parents in the earthquake. Yveline and all of Haiti will need our help and love for a long, long time.

After returning from Haiti, Tiffany told me that she went there to help, but since then she has realized her mission was not to just help, but to love the Haitians. She said the First Letter of John summed it all up: "Since God has loved us so much, we too should love one another." Loving our neighbor is an essential part of our faith . . . and the Haitians are truly our neighbors who are in desperate need of our help and our love. Tiffany delivered both.

One little footnote to this story. I think it is a wonderfully hopeful sign that a young person like Tiffany can make such a huge sacrifice and walk away from her life in order to give herself so fully to people in need. I asked her how she was able to be away from her job for a week. She said she had to use a week of her vacation time. She told me, "But it was well worth it—couldn't imagine spending it any better!!" And I understand many of the medical team that went to Haiti also used their vacation time to be of help to the victims of the earthquake.

All the medical team that came to Haiti willingly entered a world of suffering. Archbishop Oscar Romero, who gave his life for the suffering poor of El Salvador, said, "To each of us Christ is saying: If you want your life and mission to be as fruitful as mine, do like me. Be converted into a seed that lets itself be buried. Let yourself be killed. Do not be afraid. Those who shun suffering will remain alone. No one is more alone than the selfish. But if you give your life out of love for others, as I give mine for all, you will reap a great harvest. You will have the deepest satisfactions." The doctors and nurses buried themselves by unselfishly giving up their own comfortable life out of love, and they reaped a great harvest of healing . . . and went home deeply satisfied. Their being in Haiti transformed the gospel into a living word of good news to the abandoned poor. The great paradox of the gospel is that we must choose to die to self in order to live for God in Christ.

Homeward Bound

Late Tuesday afternoon (January 26) I sat in the open courtyard near the main entrance of the hospital that serves as the triage area where the incoming injured are evaluated and given some initial care. I was thoroughly exhausted from crisscrossing Port-au-Prince most of the day, capturing so many distressing images of suffering humanity amid total destruction. There was one particularly intense scene of desperation in Cité Soleil; a convoy of trucks with food rumbled down the main street causing a scene of mass bedlam as people rushed off to wherever the truck would be stopping to dispense the much-needed food. The intensity of the starving horde of people rushing past us was frightening. As I sat in the triage area trying to steal a moment of stillness amid the cacophony of woeful sounds, I scribbled down some random thoughts.

> *There is a constant buzz of noise: cries, screams, conversations in many different languages. And there is a constant whirl of movement. Nurses and doctors rushing here and there. Patients being carried in or out on stretchers. Supplies coming in. Volunteers coming and going. Constant movement and noise, day in and day out, without relief or any sign of abatement. Even at night surgeries are performed and the sound of moaning continues. I've been here five days and I can't even recall what normal life is, what it is like to walk across the street from the San Damiano Foundation office to get an espresso at the Cuban-American café that I love so much. Will normal life ever return after seeing a charred skeleton trapped beneath a hotel, or the decaying foot of a child sticking out of the rubble of a collapsed grammar school, or the bleeding wound of an amputee?*
>
> *So much suffering, yet so much compassion.*

This will sound hard to believe, but it is true: most people in Haiti will go their entire lives without ever seeing a doctor. Once all the international relief doctors working around the clock treating all the traumatic injuries go home, who will fill the gap? Haiti graduates only about eighty new doctors every year, a woefully inadequate number to meet the need. And to make matters worse, the country's main nursing school and the state medical college were both destroyed. There is no quick fix to the daunting problems facing Haiti, and countless doctors and other professionals will have to make repeated trips to this tortured island for it to have any chance of a normal life.

We were scheduled to return to the States on Thursday (January 28). On Monday and Tuesday, some of the team began to wonder about the details of our exit strategy. The guy from CURE International on the ground who greeted us upon our arrival, an amazing man with an abundance of "street smarts" who knew how to get things done in the chaos of a disaster, had left Haiti on Sunday after more than a week of being the glue that held the hospital together. None of the doctors or nurses had a clue to our departure strategy.

I woke up on Wednesday morning with the thought that I should slow down my pace on our final full day in Haiti. I decided I would not try to cram in another trip downtown. I had already truly pushed the envelope in terms of putting myself in vulnerable and dangerous situations. Moreover, I was so exhausted from carrying all the video and 35mm camera equipment everywhere I went, I felt on this last day I would simply take the still camera with me to the hospital and concentrate on just capturing gentle moments of humanity and the faces of as many patients as possible. I hoped the day would be more reflective, perhaps including a little time in some quiet corner (if I could find one) to pen some reflections.

Had it not been for the generous hospitality of Pierre and Joelle Coupad, I doubt I would have survived this trip. The last three nights were a pleasant relief from the nonstop intensity of the hospital. No rushing on this last day; I would even take a slow, leisurely walk up the hill to the hospital. I was just a few steps out of the door when the daughter was backing down the driveway. "I'm going to the hospital, want a ride?" I almost said no, but seeing as it was already hot at 8:15 in the morning I said sure and got into the car.

As we approached the main entrance I spotted an old, small school bus. As we drove past it, I noticed it was filled with members of our team, and it appeared as if a few were frantically waving at me. I figured someone had arranged for them to go on a tour of downtown. I quickly panicked as I heard them shout: "We are leaving for the airport now!!!"

Sometime Tuesday evening, a decision had been made to leave a day early because there would be no open flights out on Thursday, but there were three departing on Wednesday. We had no idea when the flights would depart or their various destinations. We just had to hope that there would be enough empty seats between the three flights to accommodate the eighteen members of our team scheduled to go home. The size of the team leaving was reduced because a couple of doctors decided to stay another week, and two had left early to go to a hospital in Santo Domingo.

The new coordinator on the ground had no way to get in touch with me. They just hoped I would show up before the bus departed. Tiffany, the young nurse from Chicago, insisted, "We can't leave without Gerry." They had a backup plan in case I missed the bus. They arranged for a car to take me separately. I pleaded with them to wait for me while I ran back to the house and packed my stuff. "It will take me two minutes, please don't leave without me." I jumped into the car, and the driver zoomed down the dirt road. The house was on the way to the airport. I was having a panic attack as I frantically shoved my clothes into the suitcase and jammed the cameras, batteries, chargers, and tapes into the padded camera bags. I gave Joelle a hug and kiss and thanked her profusely for allowing me to stay with her family. And then I rushed to the car just as the school bus arrived. To save time, the coordinator and I stayed in the car and the school bus followed us to the airport. I was teased mercilessly as "the little boy who always wandered away" and that I was the only one who had an air-conditioned ride to the airport.

The drive to the airport was relatively smooth and much quicker than we imagined it would be, as checkpoints on the road to the airport filtered out unnecessary traffic. In the space of our time in Port-au-Prince you could see some sense of order was beginning to emerge out of the cauldron of chaos. The daily charter flights ferrying aid workers arrived and departed from a small one-room cargo terminal about a mile away from the frenetic activity of the main terminal. We entered the building around 9:30 a.m., and the wait began. There were no drinks or food in the building, and it was suffocatingly hot. The exhausted doctors and nurses found spots on the floor. Using their suitcases as pillows, many fell asleep.

About an hour after we arrived, the first prop-jet landed. We soon learned there was no room on it for any of us, and so we watched it depart around 11:30 a.m. Around 1:00 p.m. the second plane landed, and thankfully we were told there was room on it for all of us. The U.S. Air Force called out the names of fifteen people on the flight, all of whom had to have their bags hand-inspected. As the boarding time approached, we were told we needed one person to volunteer to wait for the third plane. A gracious, older doctor quickly said he would wait.

After a five-hour wait in the brutally hot terminal, we boarded the plane at 2:30 p.m. and took off a half hour later. We landed in Fort Pierce, Florida, at 5:30 p.m. In Florida, six members were whisked off to nearby West Palm Beach Airport for flights that evening to Atlanta and Chicago. The remaining dozen of us would be taking a chartered plane to Dallas at 9:00 p.m. Dallas was home to eight of us, and the remaining four, including myself, would catch flights on Thursday morning from Dallas/Fort Worth Airport for three cities in California.

With a few free hours, the Dallas-bound people all had dinner at a nearby seafood restaurant. And after a week of living on Pop-Tarts everyone was hungry for a good meal. At dinner the conversation revolved around medical discussions, reliving hard or sad cases, and the administrative problems that arose from so many medical teams from around the world trying to cope with supply shortages and learning how to work together under such dire circumstances. I learned that one patient died of tetanus. And another patient who had been quarantined with tuberculosis passed away after two days of isolation. Not having much to add to the conversation, I slowly tuned out and became lost in the sudden and surreal transition from the desperation of Port-au-Prince to the exuberance of an upscale restaurant in Fort Pierce. There was so much food . . . huge steaks, a wide variety of seafood, and a steady flow of drinks. There were big-screen TVs and lots of loud conversations and laughs throughout the restaurant. It was hard to take it all in, and oddly enough, even though I was glad to be out of Haiti, I also wished I was back there.

When we arrived at the airport for the 9:00 p.m. flight to Dallas, we were surprised to find a Gulf Stream Five private jet waiting for us. One of the doctors said the plane was the top-of-the-line corporate jet. As we boarded the luxuriously appointed plane, we were each handed a yellow rose. There was a banquet of eloquently designed trays of food and an abundance of beers from around the world. During the flight we were served hot shrimp wrapped in bacon. Along the way to Dallas, we learned that the plane belonged to a wealthy and famous Texas oilman who simply wanted to help us get home and who wished to remain anonymous. In the space of a few hours I went from the extreme of desperation, destruction, and poverty to the extreme of immense wealth. The kind gesture was overwhelmingly dissonant and unsettling in my spirit, and it was a transition I could not make. I could not get the images of all I had captured on film and tape out of my head.

Early on Thursday morning, before leaving the hotel for my flight to Burbank, California, I read a passage from Elie Wiesel's book *Night*, which was quoted in a book on the Franciscan understanding of God's humility that I was reading:

> *The SS hanged two Jewish men and a youth in front of the whole camp. The men died quickly, but the death throes of the youth lasted for a half an hour. "Where is God? Where is he?" Someone asked behind me. As the youth still hung in torment in the noose after a long time, I heard the man call again, "Where is God now?" And I heard a voice in myself answer, "Where is he? He is here. He is hanging there on the gallows."*

My thoughts after reading that drifted back to the painful memory of the collapsed grammar school. I could see inside a classroom. The blackboard, small desks, scattered books and notebooks were clearly visible. The haunting sight of a young boy's decaying foot sticking out from the rubble was almost more than I could bear. One minute the boy was studying, the next minute he was dead. Where was God? God was hidden in the rubble, the magnificence and mystery of God's humanity at its worst. God was in the rubble suffering too. I thought how God is often buried under the rubble of our lives,

buried under so many trivial and unimportant things that prevent us from loving God. And loving God is of paramount importance in the life of a Christian.

I'm not sure how long it will take to make any sense out of what I saw in Haiti. Maybe it will never make any sense. But I do know that the presence of so many wonderful men and women who rushed into this hell of suffering was truly inspirational, for they became living symbols of the compassion God calls each of us to embody, even in the smallest details of our personal lives.

I do think God is hidden in the rubble. But God is also visibly present in the arms that pull someone out of the rubble. God is in the messiness of human life, reaching out in love to lift us from the rubble of our lives, rubble created by our faults, failures, and mistakes. I made a mess out of most of my life, made lots of bad decisions and succumbed far too often to my weaknesses. But God was there, even if I was unaware. Even when a person becomes more deeply aware of God's presence and makes a sincere effort to become more fully united with God, progress is usually very slow, so slow some give up along the way. In his book *New Seeds of Contemplation*, Thomas Merton writes, "It is more ordinary for the spirit to learn contemplation from God not in a sudden flash but imperceptibly, by very gradual steps. As a matter of fact, without the groundwork of long and patient trial and slow progress in the darkness of pure faith, contemplation will never really be learned at all." Patience is in short supply in our society. Try surfing the internet on a computer with a dial-up connection and see how impatient you are. Haiti's recovery will be very slow and will take a very long time. As in the life of faith, there will be no quick fixes in Haiti. All we know is God is there and God wants us there.

Hidden in the Rubble

I caught the 6:45 a.m. shuttle van from the hotel to the airport. As I passed through the security check, I began to cry. Tears just came. Part of me was still in Haiti, still seeing the carnage. When my assistant booked the flight, he used my accrued mileage to bump me to first class in hopes of reducing my stress. But there really was no stress. After Haiti, what could I possibly worry about? During the 9:15 a.m. flight to Burbank, I scribbled the following in my notebook:

> *Over the last dozen years, in many books and films, I've made lots of statements about spirituality and poverty. As I fly from Dallas to Burbank on the last leg of a long journey back from hell . . . I wonder about the value (and even the meaning) of anything I've written. Part of me feels like shutting down the San Damiano Foundation and moving to Haiti or Uganda or Peru or Philadelphia and work with Fr. Tom or Laurie or Dr. Tony or Fr. Mike. Another part of me wants to live a solitary life of monastic simplicity and stillness in a hill town near Assisi. I'm tired of filming suffering yet it is what I feel called to do. But what can I say about what I filmed in my six days in Haiti.*
>
> *As I wrote the last sentence, the woman seated next to me began laughing out loud at a scene from a film she is watching on*

her computer. Maybe the film is funny or maybe it is the three vodka and orange juices she has consumed before eleven in the morning that makes it funny. She told the flight attendant she is going to play golf as soon as she gets to California. For me what was once normal is no longer so.

The original title of my film was *A Beggar of Love.* I changed the title because it was a bit too obscure for a film on Haiti; it referred, of course, to God, but you wouldn't know that from the title. Maybe I am also a beggar of love. Do I do what I do—direct the films, write the books, speak at churches and schools—to prove that I am lovable? Am I a beggar of love pleading to be loved?

Vodka and golf . . . pain and suffering . . . loving and laughing. What does it all mean?

Is God still hidden in the rubble of my life?

Part III

After the Earthquake

An Unopened Envelope

A few days after returning from Haiti, I was having a tough time processing all I had seen. When Dr. Greg Bellig and I were at the ruins of the cathedral, I photographed an unopened envelope lying in the rubble that was addressed to a priest. After I returned home I read a story about the numbers of priests killed in the earthquake, including the sixty-three-year-old archbishop of Port-au-Prince, Joseph Serge Miot. I sent Greg an e-mail about the priest to whom the letter was addressed telling him I read he was killed in the earthquake. In his response, he wrote: "I've not stopped thinking about our time in the hospital and time on the ground around the city. It was unimaginable and forever imprinted in my memory and soul. Much that I think about is how I want to live my life differently as a result of the suffering I've seen and felt." This is precisely why it is important to spend time with the poor and the suffering. They truly change our perspective on life . . . for the better. I can't wait to return to Haiti; everything in Burbank seems trivial, and the talk revolves around Jay Leno and *The Tonight Show* host controversy.

Geological Consent

In 1926, the American philosopher Will Durant wrote, "Civilization exists by geological consent, subject to change without notice." The earthquake in Haiti is a chilling example of the validity of that statement. But the earthquake and the deadly series of recent floods in Haiti are not simply natural disasters, because civic and ecological mismanagement was as instrumental in the large loss of life as the forces of nature. It is estimated that earthquake damage and loss of life are usually ten times worse in underdeveloped than in developed nations. Most of that is because of abysmally poor building standards, which are condoned by corrupt authorities.

The damage and loss of life from the floods in Haiti were intensified because so much of the forest cover had been stripped bare for fuel. Added to Will Durant's observation is the reality that human attacks on the environment compound those from geology and climate. There will be more earthquakes, more tropical storms; they are part of life and death. But it is our responsibility to work together and do all we can to mitigate the damage by building safer homes for the poor and treating Mother Earth with utmost respect and not plundering her resources for the sake of expediency or profit.

Rising Out of the Rubble

The earthquake spawned a tsunami of suffering. During my second trip to Haiti I saw an unimaginable amount of anguish; it truly broke my heart and left me feeling useless. I did not know how to even begin to process suffering on such an extensive level. Human suffering visits every life. We live with it, endure it, try to get through it . . . and we do all we can to avoid it yet we can't. Suffering is impossible to ignore. If we try to grapple with it, it proves far too perplexing to understand. Every religion tries to address it. Christianity is built upon the suffering and death of Christ. Some try to explain suffering by simply saying "it's God's will" or "God's ways are not our ways." That certainly doesn't help relieve suffering's existential pain.

Suffering does not render itself to easy answers. However, suffering can move us from self-preoccupation to a much greater mystery. Suffering gets our attention and can lead us to a truly humble form of prayer that seeks an understanding more than a cure, seeks consolation in a subconscious hope and in an implicit faith. In suffering we are more fully connected to Christ. God in Christ understands our whole experience from the inside and we in turn can share to some extent in the divine knowledge hidden inside of Christ. Through our own suffering we become more aware of the suffering of others and more conscious of the mystery of the whole body of

Christ and our personal connection to it. Our suffering can move us from our self-centeredness to a greater sensitivity to the suffering all around us, and as a result we may begin to mirror the self-emptying love of Christ. None of this justifies suffering or makes it something good in and of itself; but it does help us, at least a little, to see some positive meaning in it. In Haiti, only through the eyes of faith can we see hope and envision something beautiful rising out of the rubble.

I Am Humbled by These People

One person in Haiti who truly made an indelible impression on me was Father Tom Hagan. For me, he is a hero among heroes. Without his help I could never have gotten in (and, more important) out of Cité Soleil during my first trip in December. I was delighted that I was able to connect Father Tom with Tom Roberts, and as a result the following letter from Father Tom to Tom Roberts was posted on NCR's website on February 2 and appeared in the print edition of the newspaper on February 5. Here it is, along with Tom's introduction:

> *Fr. Tom Hagan, 68, a member of the Oblates of St. Francis de Sales, is the founder of a nonprofit organization, "Hands Together," which began in 1985 when Hagan, then a chaplain at colleges in southeastern Pennsylvania, started taking students on visits to Haiti. Out of those visits grew a network of supporters and a respected relief organization. Hagan moved to Port-au-Prince in 1997 where he oversaw a program he had begun in Cité Soleil, that city's largest and most desperate slum. The program is widely recognized as one of the most effective educational and health organizations in that area.*
>
> *Tom Roberts, NCR's editor at large, contacted Hagan by e-mail and asked him about his experience during the quake and his assessment of the future of Haiti and the church in that country. His response arrived by e-mail Jan. 24th. With minor editing, the e-mail follows.*

Dear Tom:

Sorry my first response did not get through! My setup here

is a laptop on the ground next to a very loud electric gas generator and with what seems to be a thousand young all wanting to use the computer. I will try again.

This past week has been terrifying. I have lived through all the violence in Cité Soleil over the past years: being shot at and having guns held to my head, seeing people close to me down here shot, but none can compare to the horror of the earthquake. Doug Campbell, who has been with me for over 20 years and serves as the executive director of Hands Together, had just arrived. We were to meet with the archbishop the next morning about the situation in Cité Soleil.

Doug and I were sitting down talking when the quake began. I tried to get under a table that was only a few feet away but the floor was moving in the opposite direction. I felt totally disoriented and fortunately one of the young Haitians ran back into the house and grabbed me and Doug. There was almost total darkness and I could hear screaming but also singing, which seemed weird to me, but I was told that the people were praying.

I looked up at the rubble that was our house for volunteers, seminarians and street kids. I was bleeding from the head and there was a terrific pain in my back. Doug ran back into the rubble to try and begin to pull people out, but then we heard cries that the gas was leaking and that there would be an explosion. One of the street kids, Makenson, who was shot and is now blind and whom I found two years ago literally in the street, was crying out to me beneath all the rocks and debris but we could not get to him. [Makenson was eventually rescued.]

It was then that two ex-gang members from Cité Soleil ran up to me and carried me to Mother Teresa's nuns. When I entered their compound they were already treating the wounded and they bandaged me up and I hobbled back to my place.

Throughout the night we held vigil, and slowly we were able to get everyone out except two of the 21 seminarians who were living with me in the house. I remember vividly that night seeing people who were burned badly by the electric wires that had fallen everywhere. The next night we were all huddled outside when we would experience a very large aftershock.

It was very frightening. On the same night at about midnight we began to hear screaming and people were screaming that there was a tidal wave coming. We all started running, and for the next hour I, along with thousands of people, were moving to higher ground. We did not know what to believe.

I am ashamed to say that I am still frightened, but now I am also experiencing a feeling of being overwhelmed. When I go through Cité Soleil now I see the eight schools that we built (schools that were totally free and the only free schools like that in the country with more than 9,000 kids). I walk past what was once our clinic that took care of 20,000—again the only totally free clinic in the area. I see what once were the houses that we built for 150 people and the elderly projects for over 800. I look at the large kitchen area where people prepared hot meals each day for over 10,000—and all of it is gone.

There is also the problem of the destroyed prison, from which over 4,500 men were freed. They all escaped, and there is a side of me that is happy that they did. Many of them should never have been there. I would visit the prison every week and there were as many as 600 in one holding cell and many of them had never even been in front of a judge. Unfortunately, some are psychopaths, and all of them are now back in Cité Soleil.

I just came from offering four Masses. Each time I would finish, another crowd would come up and ask for Mass. This is a real comfort to me and more than ever I realize that I, we, can't survive if we do not simply put everything into God's hands. I've got to work hard to practice this.

Tom, you ask about the church. Well, the people here lost a very holy man [Archbishop Joseph Serge Miot] and a very good bishop, especially one who was supportive of me in Cité Soleil. He was a good friend, and I will miss him greatly. But the church will survive.

It is during a time like this that I find myself very proud of my church. Everywhere you go, you will see the church reaching out now and helping the people. The Missionaries of Charity (Mother Teresa's nuns) are just amazing. The people here have a great faith. When I go to Cité Soleil now, as I do every day, I see few tears. The people have an amazing resiliency. Maybe it is because they have few material possessions and apparently their happiness does not depend upon possessions. The sight of a sunset means more to them than their possessions. What makes me most proud of my church is that the message we give the people is that they have enormous worth in the eyes of God and that they are infinitely loved and that this terrible disaster is in no way a punishment from God.

I recently said this in a sermon and the people all stood up and began clapping and cheering. I had to ask the altar server why they were clapping (I thought that I had said something wrong because my Creole is not good) and he said, "Father, no one ever tells them that they have worth."

The Catholic Church will survive, and I am sure of it.

But the longer I am here, the less I know. I really could not speak with much authority about what will happen with the government or even what would be the best way to help the people. I also struggle a great deal even being here. I feel strongly that we can do a great deal of harm with the best intentions when we begin to be the benefactor.

Even with all this aid coming in, we must go slowly, and every step of the way we must include the Haitians in the decision making.

During these very difficult days, I find myself really loving these people. These are the same people who endured the slave ships, a horrible system of slavery, and who would be the ones who would eventually defeat Napoleon. They would continue to suffer greatly but they have a strength that is remarkable. I am humbled by them and privileged to be with them.

Pray for me. Take care!

Tom Hagan, OSFS

An Act of Spiritual Sacrifice

On the morning Father Tom's inspiring letter was published, I learned there was a chance for me to return to Haiti during the following week on a military cargo flight. I felt a rush of excitement as I submitted some required documentation. Within days of the earthquake, I had posted a nine-minute-long clip of footage from Cité Soleil that I shot in December. I titled it: "The Disaster Before the Disaster." Nearly six thousand people viewed the clip over the following weeks. As we viewed the footage from the second trip, we assembled two more clips, one featuring video and the other still photography and posted them on YouTube. Within days more than two thousand people viewed the images.

Early Friday morning (February 5), I received a call informing me that our names were not going to be on the flight manifest. And so the door back to Haiti closed. In that moment, I felt a sense of relief, knowing I was too exhausted to enter back into the nightmare of Haiti. Moreover, I was exhibiting clear signs of posttraumatic stress disorder, which perhaps was exacerbated by continual viewing of the footage as we began to edit the film. Still during the following weekend, I felt a keen sense of disappointment at not being able to get right back into Haiti. I experienced a deep emptiness and sadness that not even the New Orleans Saints' stunning upset over the Indianapolis Colts in the Super Bowl could chase away. During the game, the announcers stressed over and over again how each team had an outstanding player from Haiti. Amid the clutter of frivolous commercials costing advertisers millions of dollars for thirty-second ads, there was one short pitch for people to automatically donate $10 to the Red Cross by simply calling a special number. In the buildup to the big game, it seemed as if the entire country was rooting for the Saints in hopes the jubilation of an implausible victory would put an end to the stigma of Katrina and its long, slow recovery. There will be no such rallying point for the people of Haiti in five years. The Super Bowl has become a celebration of materialism, a high holy day of our secular culture. Lent will begin soon, a sure reminder that when we personally abstain from the material excess which modern culture offers us, we are offering a meaningful act of spiritual sacrifice. And rebuilding Haiti will take extreme levels of physical and spiritual sacrifice. I fear the world's interest will fade long before the job is done.

I'm a Bit Down

The day after his letter was posted on the NCR website, Father Tom called me. It was late in the afternoon; I had been trying to reach him all day. The soft, gentle way he said, "Hi Ger," was out of harmony with the tremendous turmoil of his day. I asked him how he was, and he said, "I'm a bit down." He told me he had been delivering food in Cité Soleil when a riot erupted during which machetes were flashed. The people were desperate to get the food. He said the bedlam was his fault because he should have covered the bags of rice in his van so no one could see them before he reached a safe place for distribution. He said that many of the convicts who fled the collapsed prison had taken up residence in Cité Soleil and had already killed three people. He said he was afraid to send his staff into the slum because they were so readily identified with him. I asked about the schools because his letter to Tom Roberts wasn't exactly clear if the buildings had collapsed, and I had heard reports the schools were not damaged. He said the schools were still standing, but under closer inspection by the army corps of engineers it was determined that they were too unsafe to enter. He said he was sleeping in a tent near the rubble of his home. Tucked also safely behind the compound's wall were some homeless kids and a doctor and his family who were living in a truck parked on his property. He also said he was worried about what will happen when the rains come, making an already intolerable situation even worse. He said he knew there were tents at the airport, but getting them to the unsheltered who desperately needed them was another story.

A few days later, in an e-mail to friends and supporters, Father Tom said that five teachers and two students from his school were killed in the earthquake.

Naked before the World

On Sunday, February 7, I received an e-mail from Carla, the wonderful woman who served as our location manager during our week of filming in December. She handled everything for me, from arranging for the hotel, to meeting us at the airport and providing transportation every day as we combed the then vibrant Port-au-Prince for images that captured not only the poverty of the city but also its colorful culture and great beauty. Carla, who is fluent in French, Creole, and English, was at her best when helping us interface with the local people. After living in Haiti for more than twenty years, she knew the country very well and loved the people. I will share just two paragraphs from her long e-mail addressed to family and friends who had bathed her in good wishes and prayers since the moment of the earthquake turned everyone's life upside down. On the second day of my second trip to Haiti, I was walking through the triage area of the hospital, kind of lost in thought over all I was seeing, when suddenly I heard a voice yell out my name, "Gerry!" It was Carla, and she was rushing toward me. We embraced for a long time, before I asked what she was doing at the hospital. She was volunteering as a translator, helping the doctors and nurses communicate with the patients. Carla and her husband live outside of Port-au-Prince and their home was undamaged, and has since become a refuge for many of her friends.

Our home has been full, our guesthouse full, our yard full, always in a constant flux of different folks knowing they have a refuge with us and yet wandering the remains of buildings and places looking for family or friends. Now there is the wonder of what next, where will the next day come from, not only the next mouthful, but what thing will be there to hang a life onto in the world out there after you wake up. The three basics of any structure for a society have fallen, the state, the church and the schools, what's left are just dreams. How it will all unfold is the question, will the world just take over the country and the Haitian way of life evaporate the way Port-au-Prince has? Will there be Haitians left after those who can leave do? The presidents of Senegal and of Benin have opened their doors to Haitians, offering land for free. Welele, the young man who has lived with us for the past four years or so, is ready to go, he says after 200 years of not getting it together, it's time to leave. The country is naked before the world, the corruption and lack of vision of her leadership is clear as the dust settles and the world stands stunned at the devastation that Haitians themselves have known they've been living in for a long, long time even before the quake.

Near the end of the e-mail, Carla shared this wonderful reflection.

There is one story that has given me inspiration. There are so many stories of survival going around, especially as they kept finding people alive underneath the rubble after so many days. One last one was a young person, I didn't hear the story myself, though many people heard it on the radio, was pulled out and still alive after more than 14 days. When asked how did they make it for so long, the young person responded by saying that every day an old man in white with a long beard came and gave them a piece of bread and sugar water! However you want to understand it, it is a story of faith. This is my inspiration at this point because it feels like we are under the emotional, spiritual, psychological rubble of despair and only as we keep the lines open to the source of all life will we be able to survive all of this! It'll be the only way to keep going by getting our spiritual bread and water of life every day under the rubble.

In the Middle of All the Deaths

I would never begin making a new documentary without months of deep thought and careful preparation. Beginning a new film is not something you rush headlong into. I personally have to really want to make a film before I begin, because before it is finished I will run out of everything—money, time, energy—and only my passionate belief in the film will fuel its completion, no matter the obstacles, no matter what resources I am lacking. Before I ever pick up a camera, there is an intense period of deliberation.

Yet when it came to the film upon which this book is based, just weeks before I landed in Haiti for the first time, I virtually had no idea I would spend the better part of the next year of my life (and probably well beyond that) consumed with Haiti.

As I mentioned in the beginning of this book, it all quietly began in an Episcopal church in Pasadena, California, where I heard an unforgettable homily on compassion. Weeks later when I landed in

Haiti, all I had was a vague idea I would do a film about compassion and it would be set in Haiti. And the first place I visited, Cité Soleil, was the worst place in Port-au-Prince. And that dreadful place has haunted me ever since. I filmed the daylights out of the city, capturing everything from the choking traffic to the magnificent sunsets. I even filmed the city from a helicopter, circling the Presidential Palace and the National Cathedral.

Slowly, I began to have an idea where the film would go. Quickly, the idea I had was crushed in the earthquake . . . and I suddenly found myself back in Port-au-Prince and in a cityscape that looked like Dresden, Germany, after it was leveled by Allied bombs.

On February 8, as I was making plans for my third visit to Haiti, I suddenly had an idea. My original plan for this upcoming trip was to land in Haiti on March 18 and stay for ten days. I felt I needed that much time to truly document the life in some of the many refugee camps. But as I glanced at the calendar, I happened to notice that April 4 was Easter Sunday. A lightbulb went on in my head. This journey to Haiti began in Advent and would end in Lent. How fitting it would be to end the film with an Easter Service in a place like Cité Soleil or some large, crowded refugee camp. As we celebrate the Resurrection of Christ, we would be embarking on the resurrection of a city in ruins. And just as I was trying to decide whether to delay the trip a week in order to be in Haiti on Easter, I received an e-mail from a friend saying he had attached a Lenten reflection by the Episcopal bishop of Haiti, Jean Zaché Duracin, which he titled "I Look at This as a Baptism." Here it is:

> *January 12th was a terrible day for the Haitian people. The earthquake left not a soul untouched. There is not a single family that did not lose a close friend or member: Mothers, fathers, siblings, in some cases entire families disappeared.*
>
> *As for resources, we have next to nothing. The wreckage is beyond imagination. However, this situation delivers us into faith. I look at this as a baptism. We who are still alive have had the blessing of survival, but in many ways we have died to the ways of the past. We have the opportunity to rise up and start anew. In this moment of grief and mourning, life must continue.*

During this Lenten season, it is important for us in Haiti to turn inward and rediscover all that is just within us. It is imperative that we be reborn in this moment. We will live without the physical trappings of the church because we still have the same spiritual guidance, the confessions, the conversations, the reflections.

We need faith. We must go forward with confidence and hope. The Haitian people are fighters. We will not give up. We must see within this situation the possibilities that exist. Jealousy, anger, hatred— this is not the time for these. We turn to Jesus Christ, who did not fall into temptation; though he was in hard situations, he overcame death in victory.

We await the resurrection of Christ as we explore what is found in this wreckage. Dear ones were lost, houses, clothes, possessions, memories—lives are reduced to nothing. The church lost precious belongings, and the physical foundation of the state is in ruins.

Yet, we Haitians are speaking to each other in new ways. We can look at each other with new eyes. We can create a society of respect and love so that we may truly live as children of God. This is how we can rebuild our country.

We have also seen how other people—other nations—love us. The people of this Episcopal Church have sent countless messages witnessing sympathy. Knowing we are not alone gives us confidence in new life. We receive comfort and consolation in our relationships.

My wife was injured in the earthquake and left to seek medical care. I cannot visit her. I miss her and wish she were here with me. It is difficult to be separated. But this separation has given me solitude and has enabled me to reflect in a new way about how to proceed in a life founded in God as a Christian.

It is natural to question, but we hold on in faith to God—God who is always good, the God of infinite compassion. That we were struck by this tragedy does not mean God is not with us. He is here. We must always remember that God lives in this world. There is pain, but there is also joy. He gives us assurance not of the life that ends, but the life that is eternal.

The earthquake did not diminish our worship, though it altered the places where it takes place. The church has not faltered and must now rise to a new role. Belief in Christ and love for our

Lord carries us into a new phase of construction. We will raise new places to worship God.

We are looking forward to a celebration of Easter; familiarity of religious practices sustains us. We give glory to God. We sing within the church of the world. We celebrate life with the same spirit we were given it. In the middle of all the deaths, there is a God of love and of life, and we must shout Alleluia with the living.

[From an interview with Bishop Jean Zaché Duracin of Haiti, conducted in French and translated by Cecily Hutton, assisting the Episcopal Diocese of Haiti and Episcopal Relief & Development in relief and recovery efforts in Haiti.]

After reading that reflection, I knew I would be in Haiti on Easter Sunday, God willing and American Airlines flying.

Birds Chirping

This morning (February 9) just before leaving for work, I spent a few minutes watching the birds and squirrels eating the seeds I put out for them. An array of birds large and small was chirping away in the early morning sunlight as they tried to compete with a greedy squirrel intent on grabbing all the seeds for himself. I love watching this feeding frenzy every morning.

As I got in my car, my mood suddenly darkened as a scene from Haiti unexpectedly rolled across my mind. I "saw" the corpses near the garbage behind the hospital. And I wept. It took me a few moments to recover before I could start the car and drive away.

How easily we drive away from unpleasant things God wishes us to heal.

But once you've been to a place like Haiti, before or after the earthquake, or any of the other countless slums and shantytowns that dot the landscape of so many impoverished nations, it is hard to walk away. Once you have seen it and felt it, it is hard to un-see it or un-feel it. I know some of the doctors and nurses from the Dallas team can't stop thinking about our time in Haiti. Tiffany and Anne Marie, the two young nurses from Chicago, are going back on March 24 for two additional weeks of service. Many are overwhelmed by conflicting emotions about their time at the Haitian Community Hospital. On the one hand they feel good about their accomplishments, but on the other hand they feel a sense of guilt over not having been able to do more or stay longer.

Out of the Dust

On February 11, a day before the one-month anniversary of the earthquake, my friend Carla wrote another e-mail update to her family and friends. Actually, the update came, and a short time later another one was sent which contained this explanation: "Sorry, we experienced a tremor while I was working on this which made the unedited version go out!" Well-meaning people can go to Haiti and try to describe or explain what is happening—just as I am doing— but nothing an "outsider" can write can compare to the feelings and insights of someone who has lived in Haiti as long as Carla has, and loves the place and people as much as she does. And so I share this poignant reflection from a wonderful woman trying to cope with the disaster that surrounds her.

> *Loved ones of ours,*
>
> *Today Feb 11th, the day before the month marker of this "event" (as it is commonly referred to now) which will begin a 3 day national time of prayer and fasting, normally the pre-carnival time 12th–14th, was one of the lowest days so far for me.*
>
> *I am deeply grateful as an undeserving human who was not buried in the rubble of a planetary shakedown. We were somehow spared even as the church just a few yards above our house crashed, pancaking on itself during those fatal seconds. Fortunately, no one was within its unsuspecting death-chamber-like walls, but I am still reeling from the truth of the real disaster as it reveals itself out of the dust.*
>
> *The ensuing chaos continues to be upon us. It almost feels immoral or unjust to me (is this survival guilt?), having been spared death, physical suffering or any loss of property through the quake but now even more so as the threatening clouds of the rainy season promise more disaster for the thousands cast out uncere-*

moniously into the streets by this catastrophic itch in the underskin of mother earth. This year those long awaited rains for the expectant farmers to plant and the welcome relief to the months of tongue-coating dust film (now mixed with cement and human remains) seem more like a death certificate awaiting those who have not been fortunate enough yet to get a tent or just a tarp. Many families are sleeping with only a cotton sheet and scraps of plastic between themselves, their children and the cold evening downpours that will surely provoke sickness and more suffering will inevitably follow.

These crushed concrete schools, churches, businesses, and homes have turned into spontaneous tombs for the irretrievable bodies of loved ones decaying in undignified circumstances. But, for me, the spiritual weight of all these instantaneously snuffed out lives is much heavier than the concrete and steel that smothers them.

The uncomfortable question as to why an earthquake could kill the horrific numbers of people compared to earthquakes of equal seismic shock was asked during the Discovery program shown the other night. As the documentary camera zoomed into the rubble of Port-au-Prince, the condemning evidence of snapped off corner posts of schools and houses where too few bars of metal and sacks of cement were used in their construction gave some hints that should make us squirm. The economic choice that parents in these types of neighborhoods are constantly pressured into making is that they literally sacrifice themselves to pay for their children's education at the expense of their own housing. This cosmic shudder exposed the worst of our human spiritual condition, stuffing a major part of humanity (most major cities have similar situations, but to a lesser degree) into indecent cracks and edges of life with no real choices. It has exposed an ancient catastrophe of racism, prejudice, exploitation and greed that exploded into this cataclysmic catastrophe of unjust proportions. There's no more hiding behind the thin curtains of laughter any more, the wails of grief have torn it away.

As I drove by a temporary shelter camp made up in a park in one of the richer neighborhoods of Pétionville the other day, I saw an older man stooping by the curb having found an unusually clean bit of water running in the gutter to scrub out his small washcloth. I *thought about not looking at him allowing him my respect for his privacy in a somewhat humiliating circumstance, but I was impelled to see him and to have him see me understanding our mutual humanity in the seconds of our passing glances. He smiled with eyes glistening into my own and cast out his hands in simple resignation.*

N a Sonje
"We Will Remember"
Carla

Another Disaster

Many of the poor in Haiti understood that education was the key to unlocking the prison of poverty which held them captive. During the long rule of the Duvaliers, there was only one state university where a college-age student could earn a degree. Since their departure many universities have opened, and some of them were actually well-run and open to talented students regardless of their financial means. But the earthquake changed all that. Haiti's best universities are now in total ruins. It is estimated that hundreds of professors and students are buried in the rubble; the exact university death toll is uncertain because most of the computer registries were also destroyed. Weeks after "the event," workers with bulldozers uncovered a classroom in which dead students were still at their desks. These were the future leaders of Haiti. The Graduate School of Technology, which was Haiti's best computer school, is gone, and the rubble is littered with crushed computers. The loss of educational opportunities is in itself another disaster. And yet another disaster is the loss of over 70 percent of the country's hospitals and clinics. Where will poor Haitians go when they are injured, sick, or disabled?

Being Present to Suffering

On February 13 I received a call from a woman in Wyoming who within hours of the earthquake began to set up her own NGO so she could organize teams of doctors from Wyoming to travel to Haiti and help the injured. Last year I gave a talk at her parish in Casper, Wyoming, and when she heard I had been to Haiti she wanted to talk with me. Her name is Jill Wamaker Hendricks. She told me she had raised $20,000 and that three teams of doctors were already on the ground working with Partners in Health, Dr. Paul Farmer's wonderful organization renowned for its progressive and highly successful means of delivering medicine in the developing world. I asked her why she was so interested in Haiti. She told me that years ago she was a member of a Pax Christi delegation that went to Haiti as an election observer. She mentioned that the pastor of Saint Anthony's Church allowed her to give the Sunday homily in order to share her plan for bringing medical help to Haiti. I asked her to send me the homily, which she did. I would like to share one short section from it, in which she discusses her first visit to Haiti.

> *A few days into my time in Haiti I reached a saturation point where my heart just broke open with grief for the poverty there. I was teary and rather withdrawn, preoccupied with trying to make meaning of what I was taking in. An older woman in my delegation, who had many years of travels to Haiti behind her, recognized the place I was in. She took me for a walk through a market place near the Presidential Palace in Port-au-Prince. She said to me, "You must put your tears aside now. Your strength is necessary here. You must be strong for these ones here." She was not comforting me. She was only giving me the facts, a wake-up call.*
>
> *There is a difference between making sense of suffering and being present to suffering. At that time, there was no making sense of it all, and there may not ever be a way of making sense of human suffering on such a scale. My friend was telling me it was time to be present to it. By being present I do not mean merely showing up and acknowledging the poverty before me, but taking part by inserting myself in the historical moment and responding where my gifts were needed.*

Two things struck me in those two paragraphs. First, she was moved to tears by the poverty she saw many years before the earthquake. This is what I have been trying to impress on people: that Haiti was a disaster before the disaster caused by the earthquake. Second, I have struggled in these pages with the topic of suffering and its meaning. I loved Jill's insightful distinction between understanding suffering (perhaps a fruitless undertaking) and being present to suffering (always fruitful) and doing something to relieve it.

This married woman with four kids saw the devastation and did something about it. She created an organizational structure to transport doctors to Haiti, found funding for it, and as a result some Haitians will be treated and all the doctors will have a life-altering experience which will forever bind them in solidarity with the poor and the suffering not only in Haiti, but everywhere.

Found and Lost and Found Again

Today (February 17) is Ash Wednesday. Lent is a journey to Easter, a journey to resurrection. I need Lent because I get busy and I forget that Christ rose from the dead. And in my fog of forgetfulness, I lose sight of how that unique event needs to have continual meaning for me, that this gift of new life still happens for me, even when I sink into despair over Haiti. But worse than forgetting, in the past I often failed to live the reality of the Resurrection, and in doing so I turned Easter into nothing more than an annual commemoration.

The gift of new life that the Resurrection of Christ gives to each of us should dramatically change the way we view the world and the way we live life. But the reality of the end of death quickly fades into a dream. Yes, we will die, but Christ forever changed the nature of death. It is no longer an ending, but a passage—a Passover—to eternal life. Yet I forget, distracted by a thousand things, 995 of which are trivial. Christ made us partakers of His resurrection; that is the core of the Christian faith. But, sadly, it is not the core of my daily experience.

Living a life of "faith, hope, and love" seems virtually impossible because of our inherent weaknesses. God continually asks us to put Him first, and seek Him at all times and in all things. We want to put God first, but we are busy, engulfed in so many distractions and preoccupations that we forget and we fail to do it. And our forgetfulness makes it easy for sin to sneak back into our lives. Slowly, the new life of Christ recedes back into the old life of man. We become shallow and stingy. Joy loses its smile and our faces turn dismal. Life loses its meaning; everything becomes pointless. God has left the building . . . or so we think. But no, God never leaves. It is we who turn our backs on God, and step by step walk farther away. Until Lent rolls around and prompts us to turn around and begin our journey back to God. The God we found, but lost . . . and who mercifully gives us an endless number of second chances to find Him again. Lent helps me see and taste the new life in Christ I so easily betray. Lent is a time to repent and return to the Source and Sustainer of life.

Lent helps me find what I have lost. Lent helps me fall in love again.

The Desert Within

This Lent, for me, will be filtered through the reality of Haiti. With so much suffering and hardship on my mind, Lent seems different this year. It seems as if the last month has been a penitential season of sorts, a time of purging old ways, and refocusing on what is truly essential.

According to the Gospel of Mark, the Spirit drove Jesus into the wilderness. Is the Spirit driving me into the desert? Seems like lots of things are driving me, but I rarely feel the Spirit driving me. Lent is a time the church sets aside for making space for the Spirit, a time to move away from the normal distractions of life and be renewed by the Spirit of Life. Lent is a time to look at what drives me, what excites me and see if those things actually drive me away from the reality of God. Lent is about empty spaces, desert places, which give me the opportunity to feel the Spirit drive me into the desert of my heart and mind in order to purge them of all those desires that are not healthy.

In the wilderness for forty days, Jesus was tempted by Satan. The desert, with its lack of clutter and people, has endless stretches of time to look closely at the wasteland of my life. The desert challenges me to come back to my true self, the self made in the image of God, an image I have tarnished by my self-destructive behavior, my yielding to the drives and desires that do not reveal the beauty of God.

The desert reveals my essential neediness and vulnerability. But the desert, with its vast horizon of empty space, is a place where I learn that I am not alone. In the desert, you find the Spirit who shows you how to be your true self.

Lent is a time to experience the peace of prayer. Thomas Merton wrote, "Only in silence and solitude, in the quiet of worship, the reverent peace of prayer, the adoration in which the entire ego-self silences and abases itself in the presence of the Invisible God to receive His one Word of Love; only in these 'activities' which are 'non-actions' does the spirit truly wake from the dream of multifarious, confused, and agitated existence."

Rice and a Couple of Beans

Anne Marie Colby is a young nurse from Chicago. She is a friend of Tiffany's; they attend the same church. She is twenty-nine years old and has worked at Northwest Memorial Hospital for the past four years, initially in the cardiac intensive care unit and presently as a labor and delivery nurse. She hopes to go to graduate school and become a nurse practitioner in the field of women's health. She sent me an e-mail on February 17 telling me she saw the Haiti footage and photographs I posted on YouTube. Then she told me how her heart yearns to return to Haiti, and that she and Tiffany are hoping to go back in mid-March.

It was late at night when I read Anne Marie's Haitian diary. It had been a long day at the San Damiano Foundation, and some people were suggesting that I was displaying symptoms of PTSD (posttraumatic stress disorder) and I needed to take care of myself. As I read her diaries, I began to cry. And that night I had a very restless, agitated sleep.

Originally, I planned to only share a few sentences from Anne Marie's diary, but in the end, I included most of what she penned . . . mostly late at night, on the edge of exhaustion, from inside a tent on the roof of the hospital. I think her depiction of what she saw and felt is remarkable. I am greatly impressed and inspired by her willingness to so mirror the self-emptying love that Christ calls us to practice. She writes:

I need to share my story with others because it was truly a life-changing experience. I fell in love with this country and its people,

and I am eager to go back in the coming months to help. I will never forget the relationships I developed with the Haitian people—they impacted me far more than I felt my presence impacted them. I hope after reading this, it will give you a little insight into what my days and nights were like in Haiti. However, nothing will prepare you until you see it for yourself.

January 21, 2010

Wow . . . is all I can say! It took 13 hours of travel to get to Haiti. As we traveled to the hospital from the airport in an old school bus, we saw people still searching under the rubble to find bodies. The look on people's faces were lifeless, no words can describe. We pulled into the long road to the hospital, and it was a disaster zone. People were everywhere, surrounding the grounds in tents, on beds, and under sheets connected to trees. There were people screaming in pain, metal rods were protruding from legs and arms, people were missing limbs, and medical workers were scurrying about running from tent to tent. This was the first vivid picture of what the next days entailed. As we stopped the truck, a crowd of people started surrounding us. We proceeded to unload our things; however, we had to be cautious because of the rise in theft.

I am overwhelmed with the sheer fact that the Haitian people are broken, hungry and are doing everything possible to stay alive. I don't blame them for stealing. The front of the hospital has a cast iron gate with one Haitian security guard with a huge gun guarding the door. Surprisingly, I never feel unsafe expect for a couple of times when the aid comes in with food. I have been up for the last 42 hours and could probably stay up more if needed. The only thing that really hurts is my feet. I still feel the adrenaline all throughout my body. There is so much that needs to be done, I feel guilty going to bed and closing my eyes for a couple of hours. We are sleeping on the roof of the hospital in a tent with other women from our team. As I look up at the sky and the stars, all I can think is . . . where am I? I hear the sounds all around me. I hear the people outside in tents, sounds of pain, crying, singing, dogs barking, roosters crowing and people talking. I am so tired, but I am committed to write in this diary every night; to document this experience, to remember that it was all real.

I was brought on this trip as a nurse to work in the OR, but ended up working in the ICU, which is where I would rather be. It is funny how things work themselves out . . . a woman came into ER/triage today. She just delivered her baby in the street and came into the hospital two hours later because she could not stop bleeding. My friend Tiffany came and got me because of my labor and delivery experience. I took her to the one private "room" and evaluated her. The baby looked okay, better than what I would think of a baby delivered on the street of an earthquake-destroyed city. I eventually found the OB/GYN physician and told him this woman's story. I told him what I thought needed to be done and he said, "Sure, do it" (he was too busy with another critical patient). I took charge, and it felt good—like I had a responsibility, a purpose, something to distract me from the insurmountable devastation. I figured everything out and stopped the bleeding. Saving one person's life for now, there are so many more.

In regards to food, I ate rice and a couple of beans and water (that was at 7 p.m.) with no lunch, no breaks, one bathroom visit. . . . It was okay. I did not complain; in fact, I barely noticed because there was no time and my body was not hungry. To tell you the truth, I can't even keep track of the time, because it is going so fast. It is non-stop . . . people coming and going. Most of the patients have some sort of trauma, crush injuries, amputations, gangrene, and infection. There is a mixture of adults and children. One of saddest things is the sound of people crying (especially the children). Some people have families and others are now orphans. This is such an incredible, life changing experience. I hope I will continue to strive to do what the Lord has brought me here to do. God—Keep me Safe!!

January 22, 2010

Soooo tired . . . I just want to sleep. We worked 18 hours today straight. No lunch or breaks, but ultimately, it didn't matter because I am not doing this for myself, but for people who really need it. What we desperately need here is more nurses!! We have enough physicians, surgeons and anesthesiologists, but we really need critical care nurses. The surgeons can do all the surgeries they want, but if we do not have the nursing staff to take care of the patients, they will die.

I sit in my sleeping bag, listening to dogs barking, some Haitian women singing prayers and some people crying. Today, we are trying to discharge people home, or to the streets. However, people will not leave the hospital, they are surrounding it on the outside and inside. We need people to go home, to make room for others, but they don't have a home and don't want to leave. I walked outside the hospital today and flies were surrounding people's wounds. Not to mention the smells: smells of infection, feces and death. These people are hungry, thirsty and sad. Their faces tell a story of fear and uncertainty of what the future may bring. I want to feed them, clothe them and hug them . . . they need love too. Love you Lord . . .

January 23, 2010

It is 2:20 am in the morning; I have been up for 19 hours straight. Some of the teams leave the hospital at 6:00 p.m. and think they are done for the day. However, the patients still need to be taken care of, we can't just abandon them. I am here for one reason—to help! I have become close with a couple of the children. Before I go to bed at night I have to make a round in their rooms to see if they are ok and are not in too much pain. One girl named Daniella would sing when she was in pain. Other children had different needs and I became so close to them that I learned what they needed instinctually and gave it to them.

Today was also the first day the banks opened since the earthquake and the lines were outrageous. The local street markets opened up as well, with women lining the streets with buckets of fresh produce from the hills lined up right next to small mountains of trash. Sanitation did not play a factor. The nation of Haiti was already poor . . . this is just going to push them into further destruction.

January 24, 2010

Another long day—we wake up to the sunlight and heat beating down on us from the roof. Tonight was my first shower in 5 days (it was like heaven). I am so thankful that I had baby wipes for the rest of the days, to wash down my body. My legs and feet are so swollen from standing all day.

Tonight the American soldiers came in with guns. They were walking around and stumbled upon us. They didn't even know we were there, so they told us they promised to send for some security in the days to come.

I keep seeing the same faces and families in the hallways. I smile and say hello and check on them. I am trying my best to show them that someone cares. A smile might not be that much, but it is what I have to give to them. This morning I was woken up by a blood curdling scream, a mother who just delivered a baby a couple of days prior brought in her baby and was told that it was dead. It was a sound I will never forget . . .

January 25, 2010

It's 2:30 a.m. and I can't keep my days straight. I believe today was our 5th day, which has just flown by. I am falling in love with these kids and the sadness is setting in. Some kids are orphans and have no one to take care of them. Their lives are forever turned upside down. The traumatic memory of seeing family members die or the pain they have had to personally endure will never leave them. The lack of food is so great; we can't feed the patients *because we aren't eating either. I have taken my own power bars or oatmeal and given it to my kids. However it is hard to give to one and not the others, so I try not to make it obvious. Trucks come and drop off supplies and food and the people outside the hospital mob each other to get it. The food and supplies are coming in and going out as fast as we get it. People are stealing the food, but I can't get upset because they are just trying to survive.*

January 26, 2010

This morning was rough in the ICU. This young woman died from what we believed to be possible TB or pneumonia. It was very sad, and it was the first time on the entire trip that I broke down. I had to leave for a little while, to catch my breath. I found some of my Cure people and we said a quick prayer for the lady. Then this man asked if I wanted to go to the orphanage for a couple of hours . . . YES—this is what I needed, just a quick break and it was so worth it. The children at the orphanage just wanted to hug you, hold you and grab onto you. The girls were all interested in my nail polish (something they had never seen) and also my freckles on my arms (they were just pointing at all of them). They were so happy, smiling and not really fazed by the earthquake despite the fact that they were all sleeping and living outside, like all of the Haitians, for fear of another earthquake. We assess them clinically and afterwards they sang us prayer songs, some in French and others in English. I started to tear up, but they were all staring at me (I had to compose myself).

Today at 5:00 p.m., we were told that we had to leave tomorrow at 6 a.m. I was shocked because I was planning on that extra day and leaving on Thursday night. Tiffany and I both want to stay another day or days, but logistics (transportation and arrangements) are hard to change. Our whole team is leaving and it is just not safe for two young women to be here alone.

I am dreading waking up tomorrow. . . . I feel like my work here is not done. I want to stay longer, but at the same time I am emotionally and physically drained. Lack of sleep, food and my growing connection with these kids is a stark contrast.

January 27, 2010

As I sit on the airplane going back to the States, I am sad. Everything happens for a reason. I was brought to Haiti for a specific purpose and I believe it was fulfilled. However I feel like I need to go back and help these people who forever captured my heart.

Time

Anne Marie reminds us that Christ is not asking us to be successful or productive. Christ is looking for us to be present . . . present to God (in prayer), and present to each other, present to each other in acts of love and mercy, especially present to the poor and the suffering.

But we don't really take Jesus seriously. We don't love our enemies. We don't turn the other cheek. We don't forgive 70 x 7 times. We don't bless those who curse us. We don't share what we have with the poor. We don't put all our hope and trust in God.

We say: I am not a saint. We say: This gospel stuff can't be meant for everybody. We say: The gospel is an ideal. But the gospel is not merely an ideal. For the followers of Christ, the gospel is the Way. Lent gives us the chance to see we have strayed from the Way.

Lent is a time for self-examination, a time for repentance, a time for acts of self-control and acts of charity through self-emptying. But mostly Lent is a time to enter into the suffering and death of Jesus which opened the reign of God's grace and eternal life to all humans.

Lent is a time for Christians to take Jesus seriously.

For the very poor, their lives are forever Lent and Good Friday. Resurrection is far from their hopes. They hope for a morsel of food.

We Are All Beggars

I know, deep down and with conviction, that one person can make a difference in the lives of many. I've seen it, filmed it, over and over again . . . in Peru, Brazil, Mexico, El Salvador, the Philippines, Jamaica, Kenya, Uganda, and in Detroit, Philadelphia, Los Angeles, and San Francisco. But the levels of poverty and suffering I've seen, especially in the war-torn north of Uganda and in earthquake-ravaged Haiti, distress me so much that I struggle to resist becoming depressed, of feeling that it is all hopeless, that the unthinkable suffering endured by countless millions will never end because of our stunning and callous indifference.

It has become hard for me to enjoy anything, because the cruel, bitter reality of poverty is always on my mind. How can I enjoy a nice meal in a restaurant or enjoy a vacation somewhere beautiful and relaxing when so many people are starving and dying every day, when so many never get a break from the prison of poverty? I know these things are good and even necessary to relieve the stress of this work, but putting the plight of the poor into some recess in my mind and not thinking about it is virtually impossible.

And I struggle with every purchase I make. I don't have much disposable income, so there is not much I can buy, but just before Christmas I convinced myself I "needed" (or at least wanted) some electronic gadget that was under $300 that would allow me to play music in my home library. I love listening to Gregorian chant while working on a film script or book; it soothes me and inspires me at the same time. When I got it home, I was unable to open the box, and came close to returning it because I suddenly thought of it as a luxury I did not need. I waited a full day before opening the box. One of my films has this very tough, demanding thought: "As long as we enjoy comfort and require security, it will be impossible to have true compassion for the poor and the weak." My films are known for those types of challenging statements . . . such as this one which is even harder: "Christ is not asking for your spare change (in response to the poor); he is asking for your very life." I wrote those lines; living them is another story.

I know very well that our nation is in the midst of an economic crisis, brought on by unbridled greed and an immoral, illegal, and unethical war in Iraq. Yet, I see, not only here in Los Angeles but also around the country when I travel to speak, very few tangible signs of economic hardship. People are in malls and restaurants, and planes are packed. It is a constant struggle for me to reconcile so much affluence, even during an economic downturn, with the chronic and severe poverty I see around the world.

So much of life today is deeply disturbing, especially our attitudes toward poverty and peace. I can't understand the irony of how we seek peace by going to war. Our impulse toward war uncovers our erroneous belief that some people are not important, that some lives, even the lives of some children (the children of our enemies), are expendable. I can't understand how we are undisturbed by the reality that more than 20,000 children die every day from preventable diseases, most stemming from hunger. The economic downturn that is dramatically damaging the lives of the poor reveals the utter lack of moral and ethical constraints on capitalism and consumerism; and the unbridled greed of commodity hucksters is nothing short of idolatry. We have become so numbed by the scope of poverty, as well as by our own self-interest, we don't even feel the pain of the other, don't realize their misery is also our misery. As a society we have failed to understand that our lives are both interior and relational, that we are designed for communion with God and each other. Our lives have become impoverished because we do not value simplicity, do not realize what is truly essential, and do not reach out to the chronically poor and rejected.

Even though it is still a struggle at times, I must be on guard not to confuse the necessities of life with what is luxurious. The humble simplicity that embodies poverty of spirit stands in stark contrast with the frenetic pursuit of comfort, power, pleasure, and riches that permeate a society that prizes possessions as a good in itself.

The emptiness we feel stems from not realizing we are made for communion with God. If we are not growing toward unity with God, then we are growing apart from God. We need to bring to Christ what we are so that in time we become what He is.

I believe personal wholeness is attained when we achieve freedom from the greedy tendencies of the ego and its insatiable hunger for possessiveness. Yet I struggle with how to be empty, willing to lose myself in order to enter into a deep and rich communion with others.

I need to escape from the distorting influences of society by checkering my life with periodic periods of solitude. Only solitude allows me to reconnect with the truth of my own nature and my relationship with God. This is where true, fulfilling joy lies.

We are all beggars. None of us is sufficient unto herself or himself. All of us are plagued by unending doubts and restless, unsatisfied hearts. By ourselves, we are incomplete. Our needs are always

beyond our capacities, and we only find ourselves when we lose ourselves. Prayer and contemplation free us from our self-serving tendencies and prepare us to lead lives of service to others without
unconsciously desiring our own success.

We live in a world of stark inequality and injustice.

So did Jesus.

Jesus had a deep concern for those who suffered and were marginalized.

So should we.

For the follower of Jesus, compassion is not an option; it's an
obligation . . . and a sign our lives have been transformed into the
healing presence of Christ.

Gentle and Lowly of Heart

Jesus asks us to be gentle and lowly of heart. But these traits are not
ones our society values. To be humble is to be seen as being weak.
When we look at the major crises we face today, both in the secular
world and within the church, we see that the absence of humility has
played a significant role. Power tends to corrupt human relationships. The powerful Wall Street bankers were unconcerned about
how their reckless actions would impact the simple and unpreten-
tious people who placed their money and trust in their institutions
or borrowed from them, people who worked hard to pay their mort-
gage and dreamed of a comfortable, secure retirement. The sexual
abuse crisis in the Catholic Church has more to do with the priest's
power than it does with the issue of celibacy. If, for instance, the
greedy Wall Street banker and the lustful Catholic priest were truly
gentle and humble of heart they would have exercised their financial
and pastoral power in a way that valued the dignity of their cus-
tomers and parishioners; moreover, the banker and the priest would
love, protect, and serve the weakest and most vulnerable in their
communities. But too many bankers and priests want to sit at the
head of the table, content to offer crumbs to those under them.

Sadly, every secular and church institution seeks to protect and
increase its power . . . by any means necessary. We live in a culture
of control, which the philosopher Charles Taylor, in *A Secular Age,*

traces back to the seventh century when society began to be seen as a mechanism which needed to be adjusted and manipulated rather than a living organism. People no longer believed in a kind, providential God, and so the powerful took God's place and imposed their will on society. Banks are not humble, and so they defrauded people of their savings. The church is not humble, and so children are abused and guilty priests are protected.

When we look at Haiti's tormented history, we see that Spain, France, and the United States never acted out of humility and always acted out of their own self-interests. The thirst for power created the evil monsters with gentle nicknames, Papa Doc and Baby Doc. And it seems clear to some that the former priest Jean-Bertrand Aristide was not humble enough to resist the temptations of power. And so, human failure and nature's eruptions have created a crisis of epic and biblical proportions.

But the Bible suggests that we need not fear any crisis, because it is through crises that God drew closer to the people. The people of Israel lost everything, including God, only to receive him more closely than they could have imagined.

The tragic situation in Haiti should not be a cause for despair. Instead it should lead all of us, Haitians and non-Haitians, into a deeper sense of authentic humility and draw us into a deeper more authentic relationship with God and each other. Hope is born in adversity.

What's happening on Wall Street and in the church—or any secular or sacred institution—is only a mirror of all of us at this present time. Forgiveness is the conduit for love, and it is the only remedy for the situation. The earthquake is a call to awareness; the next step is forgiveness, turning around, and love, building brick by brick a new world.

And so we look forward to the hope of the resurrection, in Haiti, in the world, in our communities, in our families, and in ourselves. Hope is faith in action, and it allows us to face even the most difficult problems, trusting God for a way through them. Saint Paul understood the power and resiliency of hope when he wrote: "We are afflicted, but not crushed; persecuted but not despairing; struck down but not destroyed" (2 Corinthians 4:8–9).

In these pages I have at times struggled with trying to discern what the right course of action was in regard to my returning to Haiti. Over the years at San Damiano, it has been my experience that whenever I try to make or force something to happen it fails. Especially when it comes to fundraising, which seems to work best when I do nothing more than living a radical trust in God to provide me with the resources, both in terms of people and finances, when I need to make a film. Sure, I must ask for help, but I've learned never to use any form of manipulation in order to acquire what I need.

For me, the spiritual life comes down to contemplation and action. We easily understand the action part of the equation, but contemplation does not come easily or naturally, especially in our culture which does not value stillness and silence, which are so essential to a balanced and healthy spiritual and physical life.

In the Footsteps of Saint Francis of Assisi

I think Saint Francis came to see clearly that the fundamental principle of the gospel requires that the weakest and least presentable people are indispensable to the church, and that the followers of Christ must be in communion with the poor and must be willing to love our enemies. Each of us is wounded in some way; each of us is an enemy. We need each other, and we need God. On his life's journey, Saint Francis of Assisi took his own path. He made mistakes, and some of his actions were rather irrational. Some of his ideas were outrageous. One can easily imagine him as difficult to be with, at times being downright ornery. But no matter his mood, no matter what people thought of him, he kept his focus on God. This is our challenge.

Saint Francis said the road to God is straight and narrow: the road is poverty and prayer. Far too often, I go to God with my hands full . . . and ask for more. Francis was willing to go to God with empty hands. For Francis, the only thing that really mattered was utter trust in God, and his adult life was a continual witness to the realization that total trust cannot exist until we have lost all self-trust and are rooted in poverty.

The deepest levels of self-denial which Saint Francis reached present us with a huge gap in comparison to our feeble efforts at approaching perfect trust in God. What is it that keeps me from total surrender into the loving embrace of God? I know what God seeks, yet I hesitate. I know God loves me, and this love, I realize, does not spring from a reluctant heart; God stands always willing and waiting to love us even more deeply . . . yet we hesitate in accepting God's love out of fear of losing ourselves and being buried in God.

The only way to overcome this fear and grow in trust in and love of God is through a serious commitment to prayer. In poverty, Saint Francis found a way into prayer. Nothing was more important to him than spending time in prayer. Prayer is about building a relationship with the source of Love.

For Saint Francis, prayer was the way to learn how to live love.

I have been walking in the footsteps of Saint Francis for sixteen years, and I'm only now beginning to see, albeit dimly, the connection Francis made between poverty and prayer. Contemplation leads to communion, communion with God, communion with each other and all creation. Contemplation leads to action, action that manifests and makes real God's mercy and compassion.

Contemplation and poverty are natural partners. Contemplation helps us to see, to see both inside us and to see around us. Our contemplative vision improves as our lives become more simplified. Our lives are cluttered with so much stuff, and we are so easily distracted by so many things, that our spiritual vision is severely diminished.

We live in a thick fog of materialism and escapism. Poverty and simplicity help us see what is important, help us see another's need, help us see injustice and suffering, help us see the need to be free from all attachments that limit our freedom and ability to love. We strive to amass wealth, but true wealth resides in creating fraternity.

The world is divided into two camps: the rich and the poor. And between those two camps there is no communication, no shared life, no communion. The rich and the poor are strangers, and their mutual isolation gives birth to misunderstanding and mistrust. And we end up with Haiti. And the gap between the rich and the poor grows wider and deeper by the hour. Jesus condemned the unnatural and unjust division between the rich and the poor, because the division causes pride, envy, jealousy, self-centeredness, and loneliness. The Kingdom of God, Jesus tells us, is about unity, reconciliation, harmony, peace, and love.

Contemplation and communion lead to action, call us to the margins of society, to the American urban jungles of deprivation, crime, and violence, to the dark corners around the world, where people live in massive slums of overwhelming need, clinging to life without clean water or electricity and barely enough food for survival. And in these deprived places, we not only give life, but life is also given to us . . . as Tiffany and Anne Marie experienced. It is here we see for the first time the oneness that has always been there, though obscured by our blindness.

Through contemplation we learn to see. Through communion we learn to share. Through action we learn to love. In his book *The Way of Love*, Anthony de Mello, the Jesuit priest from India who died in 1987, wrote: "It is a sobering thought that the finest act of love you can perform is not an act of service but an act of contemplation, of seeing. When you serve people you help, support, comfort, alleviate pain. When you see them in their inner beauty and goodness you transform and create."

Be still. Know God. Live love.

A Better Life Lesson

On February 23, I received the following e-mail from Dr. Greg Bellig:

> Going to serve in soup kitchens today and tomorrow with the kids instead of Disneyland. Think this will be a better life lesson. We are sending the money we would have spent to Haiti. The kids agreed.
>
> The Lord used your book [I sent him a draft of this book] to challenge my own life objectives and decisions. It is so easy to live for self instead of living out of the abundance of Christ's love in us. We want to live life to the fullest and for Him.

There Is So Much to Do

And on the heels of Greg's encouraging e-mail came a discouraging e-mail from Father Tom to his friends and supporters.

Dear All,

I am fine and doing well. I really miss my little chapel and my prayer life has suffered a bit. There is so much to do. I take each day one at a time. I took a few days away from it all which helped.

Thanks so much for your friendship and support. It is so difficult to say what we need when I know that some of the material may take such a long time to get to us. There is still no organization. There is also, unfortunately, a lot of corruption and stealing. People are desperate.

For the time being pray for us. God bless you!

Tom

My prayer life has suffered a bit too. In my presentations to schools and churches, I talk about my early morning prayer routine, spending at least ninety minutes in stillness and silence, praying the Liturgy of the Hours followed by contemplation and spiritual reading. In Haiti after the earthquake, that routine was not possible, and since my return, the first thing I do in the morning is work on this book. I think that writing this is a form of prayer . . . but if I were truly honest, it is more busyness. I cannot truly live a life of radical dependency on God if I do not spend serious time alone with God. Every day needs to include a little slice of Sabbath.

The only reason Father Tom survived emotionally, physically, and spiritually his years in Haiti is because he was vigilant in protecting his morning time of solitude with God. I can imagine the pain of loss he is suffering because of the destruction of his chapel.

Many Hands

While working on the film and book, my mind is preoccupied with my return to Haiti on March 26. I dread what I will see. I know the situation is actually getting worse for the nearly million people living in the camps without adequate shelter. On March 6, I received an e-mail from a friend who just returned from her second trip to Haiti since the earthquake. Her name is Johanna Berrigan, and she is a physician's assistant from Philadelphia. She is part of a Catholic Worker community that operates a free health clinic that works in harmony with the St. Francis Inn. I featured the clinic in my film *Room at the Inn*. I especially appreciated the way the spirituality of Saint Francis blended with the spirituality of Dorothy Day. While making the film, Johanna told me that Bishop Thomas Gumbleton, the retired archbishop of Detroit, was staying at the Catholic Worker house, located just blocks from the St. Francis Inn, and he wanted to meet me. Bishop Gumbleton insisted that I call him Tom, but it was hard for me to comply. For the past year or more, Johanna and Bishop Gumbleton have been working to establish a free health clinic just outside of Port-au-Prince. Here is Johanna's e-mail:

Dear Friends,

It is two weeks since our return from the second trip to Haiti. Tom Gumbleton, Colleen Kelly and Johanna Berrigan went back to Haiti to deliver a tent to the health agents to be used as a clinic site during this crisis, and to take more medicines and supplies. With the shock of the impact of the earthquake over, we face with the Haitian people the challenge of looking squarely at the damage, embracing the suffering, and doing what must be done in order to carry on. The situation is bleak and dismal to say the least. There is a temptation to yield to hopelessness and yet, the energetic, heartfelt determination of the Haitian people to do what they can for their community inspired us once again. Our time in Haiti was hopeful in many ways, even though ever more mind numbing [than the first trip]. It is painful to bear witness to such tragic circumstances made all the more difficult because there seems to be no clear planning for rebuilding.

It poured rain the first night that we were in Haiti this time. We were awakened many times by the sheer loudness and force of the rain against our tent. We were dry, but as Colleen Kelly so poignantly said, "It was difficult to sleep just thinking about all of those people without tents to help keep them dry." The short walk in the rain from the field to Matthew 25 house, sloshing through the mud, was sobering enough. I don't know how the Haitian people will continue to endure these discomforts and daily challenges.

At one point, we heard that there was a decision not to distribute tents. The officials determined that providing tents was not a

long term solution. It was decided that each family would be given
a tarp starting May 1st. Tom Gumbleton, who did not have tent
but a tarp draped over a bed, can tell you first hand that this is not
a solution at all. By 2:00 a.m. he was soaked.

There are major concerns for the health and well being of the
Haitian people as the rainy season approaches. In addition to the
psychological and physical suffering from the earthquake there are
now additional problems because of a serious lack of sanitation in
these areas. This along with the mounting trash and sewage backup will increase the cases of cholera, and typhoid. With the mosquitoes that the rains will bring, there will also be an increase in
the cases of malaria and dengue fever.

There is a Haitian proverb that says "Men anpil, chay pa Lou."
"Many hands make light a heavy load." This proverb describes our
journey and our efforts to secure a tent for the health agents. This
was the main purpose for returning to Haiti so soon. Through the
determined efforts of many people, we were able to ship a 500 lb
tent to the Dominican Republic. Through the efficient, kind service of Fed Ex employees, we were driven to the Haitian border with
the tent and all of our supplies. Once we arrived at the border,
Daniel organized a crowd of young people that had gathered to
help. With seemingly little effort, almost no talking, no noise, chaos
or arguing this group of young people virtually levitated the 500 lb.
tent into the van. Because of the help of these many hands from
Detroit to Haiti we now have a tent large enough to accommodate
at least 4 exam rooms. The very next day, Kay Lasante, House of
Health, was standing tall.

Sadly, during our time in Haiti, there were extremely few signs
of clean up or recovery efforts taking place. We thought that what
we had seen during our first trip was horrendous enough, only to
witness on this trip more shocking sights. Daniel drove us through
Port au Prince via Desaline Boulevard, one of the main streets in
downtown Port au Prince. We had not been on this street during
the previous trip. We saw building after building totally
destroyed—an overwhelming number. Amidst this destruction,
people are carrying on with their activities of daily life as much as
possible. It was just surreal to see people selling goods at their curb

side markets along side collapsed structures, huge mounds of concrete, and ever mounting piles of trash. I was at once filled with respect and sorrow as I watched the way the people, especially the women and children, walk carrying goods on their heads, passing by these ruins with such dignity.

We went to visit The Little Sisters of St. Therese in Carrefour. They have a sister city relationship with the Sisters of the Immaculate Heart of Mary here in the states. The earthquake caused extensive damage in the area. The elementary school was completely destroyed. Tragically, there were more than 100 children in the school at the time of the earthquake attending the afternoon session. The bodies of the children remain buried under the rubble. The smell was putrid and the sight of desks, notebooks and toys scattered around the destroyed building spoke profoundly of the lives and dreams lost. Four of the Sisters were killed along with three lay teachers. The Novitiate was also completely destroyed. Like everyone else in Haiti, the sisters now sleep outside in tents. They have received no assistance from either the government or the Church. We were at first puzzled why their Bishop had not come to visit. They explained that their Bishop was Bishop Miot, who was found dead under the rubble of the Cathedral office building the day after the earthquake. They have no idea how they will begin to clean up these sites in order to continue with their mission.

We will return to Haiti tomorrow, March 7th. We will take with us more medicines and supplies in order for them to operate the clinic on a long term basis. Our presence and the health care project in this location will bring much hope and healing during this desperate time.

Our gratitude for your concern and generosity is boundless. Please continue to pray for the Haitian people.

Peace,
Johanna Berrigan, for House of Grace Community
Bishop Tom Gumbleton
Colleen Kelly

The coming rains will drench the displaced survivors in new misery and sickness. The camps are becoming filthier with each passing day.

The stench of human waste is inescapable. Death still lingers in the air as bodies are still being pulled from the rubble almost two months after the earthquake. The government still hasn't figured out what to do with the rubble . . . or the people. More than 1.2 million people are living in scattered settlements. It is estimated that more than 17,000 children are suffering from acute malnutrition, and about 3,000 of these are severely malnourished and in need of life-saving assistance. The death toll is now estimated at 215,000; and it is believed that at least 300,000 had been injured on that dreadful day when the earth roared. It will indeed take many hands to help the people of Haiti recover from a disaster of preposterous proportions.

A Cracked System, a Shaken Psyche

Here is the lead from an article published in *The New York Times* on Saturday, March 20, 2010: "Inside this city's earthquake-cracked psychiatric hospital, a schizophrenic man lay naked on a concrete floor, caked in dust. Other patients, padlocked in tiny concrete cells, clutched the bars and howled for attention. Feces clotted the gutter outside a ward where urine pooled under metal cots without mattresses. Waking through the dilapidated public hospital, Dr. Franklin Normil, the acting director, who has worked there for five months without pay, shook his head in despair." Written by reporter Deborah Sontag, the story looks at the mental health crisis in Haiti. The inadequacies of the mental health system have been exacerbated by the earthquake. Before the earthquake there were barely more then a dozen psychiatrists in all of Haiti. And with the swiftly rising tide of posttraumatic symptoms, anxiety, depression, and psychosis, there is urgent need for outside psychiatric help.

Commercial flights to Port-au-Prince resumed two weeks ago . . . and American Airlines is flying . . . and so I'll return to Haiti in less than a week. This past week, I have shown clips from my first two trips to Haiti at two churches in Los Angeles, and both times the audience was stunned and overwhelmed by the conditions before and after the earthquake. I arrive in Port-au-Prince on March 26, the day before Palm Sunday. It is fitting to spend Holy Week in the camps. I hope to film an Easter Sunday service in a camp.

Holy Week in Haiti

Just landing in Port-au-Prince was all the proof I needed to know the situation had improved in Haiti. Gone were the clutter and chaos of giant military and relief aid cargo planes and the exodus of fleeing Haitians. The airport was calm and orderly and the immigration process was smooth, even though the lines were long. The drive from the airport to the hotel in Pétionville offered me a few signs that life was returning to normal, despite the rubble which was still piled high. The traffic, while still insanely congested, was actually moving more freely. People were out, moving about on foot, selling their goods on the sidewalks and in crowded markets. Bulldozers were clearing some of the rubble. There was music in the air. But still, there were many visible signs of extreme need. There seemed to be more tent cities. I was able to drive around more parts of the city on this trip, and I continued to be astounded by the massive scope of the destruction. The endless mountains of rubble were constant reminders of the trauma and loss endured by the Haitians . . . and they must walk past them day in and day out, meaning the memory of that horrible day never gets a chance to recede for very long.

Everywhere I went in my nine full days in Port-au-Prince, I encountered painful stories of overwhelming need and heartache. Countless people are still extremely hungry. In one small camp I visited, I met a hungry mother and her week-old son, just clinging to life. Each day is an all-consuming fight for survival. People are walking around carrying plastic bags containing all they own. One man whom I met outside the hotel and who escorted me a few times through the small camp located across the street from the hotel wore the same clothes every day. He has nothing; yet he has his dignity and sound ideas of what is needed for the situation in Haiti to improve. He was articulate, well-educated, and clear-headed . . . but he had no clear options on how to change his situation. There were no options, no work. He carried a book with him on how to become an entrepreneur, but he could only read it for a half hour at a time because his eyes became tired as a result of using reading glasses whose prescription had not been updated in years. He joined me for

breakfast and dinner on a few occasions, and for him, something to eat was an amazing blessing. He savored or saved every crumb.

It was hard to see so many hands outstretched for help, hard to hear so many pleas for food, and not be able to respond . . . beyond occasionally, and with great discretion, handing someone, usually a woman with an infant, ten or twenty dollars. However, it was wonderful to be able to respond in a more substantial and very tangible way in two situations where I saw I could offer some direct help. One day, I visited a camp where 18,000 people lived in tents. Before being able to enter the camp, I had to meet with the president of the camp and explain why I wanted to film there. During the tour I learned that there was only one toilet for every 200 people. The stench of human waste was noxious. The president wanted to dig deeper holes and more of them, but he did not have the resources to do so. I promised to try to help. Days later, I met with Sister Mary, a wonderfully dedicated nun who runs Matthew 25 House. I explained the sanitation problem at the camp. She said digging deeper and more holes was not a good idea, as it would have a detrimental impact on the surrounding soil. She told me about environmentally safe toilet systems. I asked her if she would oversee the installation of some of the toilets if I gave her the funds to buy them. She said she would be delighted to do so. I gave her a check for $2,500 from the Santa Chiara Charitable Fund. I am not sure how many toilets the money will be able to purchase, but the president was truly delighted that someone did something for the people of the camp.

On Palm Sunday I drove to the Adventist Hospital to meet up with Tiffany and Anne Marie, the two young, wonderful nurses from Chicago, who were doing their second tour of volunteer help. The plan for the day was simple: I would drive them back to the Haitian Community Hospital where the two children they formed a special bond with would be waiting for them. Of course, when I arrived Tiffany was rushing off to tend to the needs of a young patient. She asked me to come with her. I was not ready for what I would witness.

We quickly arrived at the side of a crib of an infant boy. The boy had been badly burned on most of his back and rear end. Two weeks earlier scalding hot liquid accidentally fell on him. Tiffany was briefing a replacement volunteer nurse on the procedures for treating the wound and changing the bandages. The child screamed as she slowly cut and removed the bandages. She gently placed some ointment on the wounds. It was painful to film. After the wounds were treated and dressed in new bandages, Tiffany told me she wanted me to see a true miracle.

It was the miracle of new birth . . . a very special new birth, the birth of a thirty-one-week-old premature baby, far too young to survive even in most neonatal care units in the United States.

At the time of the delivery, the mother of the baby was critically ill with preeclampsia, a medical condition that is brought on because of high blood pressure during pregnancy. The medical team feared she would develop seizures while her baby was in utero, which would cut off the flow of oxygen to the fetus, thereby suffocating it. This baby needed to be delivered immediately. As a nurse, Tiffany had no experience with labor and delivery, let alone any experience with premature babies, so she had to work fast to educate herself on potential outcomes with this tiny baby. She said, "I immediately found a book called Neonatal Resuscitation Program which basically provides algorithms (flow sheets) that direct medical care for particular situations. The book provided me the needed dosages and specific time-sensitive procedures that may occur. After reviewing the details I then called my attending physician at University of Chicago Comer Children's Hospital and discussed what I was about to encounter. I asked the physician for assistance with providing antibiotic and fluid replacement recommendations. After this discussion, I headed to the operating room ready to deliver this tiny little baby. The baby was delivered at 7:35 p.m., his color was better than expected, heart rate within normal parameters and moving his extremities appropriately. I looked at the tiny baby and said, 'Thank you, God!'"

But the baby didn't look like he was thirty-one weeks. Tiffany and the medical personnel estimated that the baby was maybe twenty-nine weeks old and weighed about two pounds. The hospital was not equipped to care for such an unstable baby. Nor was Tiffany. She said, "We did have to provide some supplemental oxygen, and by the Lord's gracious gifts He gave me, I was able to get a peripheral intravenous catheter in this little baby's hand. Because of his IV we were able to give him his necessary antibiotics and fluids. After watching him closely along with three other providers we moved the baby into the emergency department storage room. The room was the only room that provided the warmth and ability to monitor the patient closely. Because I was the only health care provider with pediatric experience I decided to stay awake with this baby the entire evening. I watched this baby's chest rise and fall for fourteen hours straight, making sure his oxygen remained in his tiny nose and his temperature remained between specific degrees. Another volunteer from the States and I created a makeshift isolette made of sheets, and a transport table with a light source squeezed between two sheets. I would monitor his temperature every thirty minutes to ensure his temperature didn't get too hot or too cold. Thinking back on this tiny baby, I am still in awe that he survived his first night and I was a witness to yet another miracle in Haiti."

I drove Tiffany and Anne Marie to the Haitian Community Hospital for their long-awaited reunion with their "kids" . . . Yveline and Daniel. According to the plan, their families would bring the children to the hospital and the nurses would take them away for a day of fun. When we arrived there was good news and bad news. The good news was that Daniel was there with his father, but Yveline was nowhere to be seen. It was such a tender moment to see Daniel and Anne Marie greet each other. They sat together in what once was the super hectic, open-air triage area. They held hands, smiled, and talked for a long time. It was beautiful to see this powerful connection that was forged in love in the middle of a disaster.

But off to the side, I saw Tiffany standing alone, sobbing. Where was Yveline? In time, Tiffany found out that the grandmother did not have enough money to take a Tap-Tap to the reunion meeting. We're talking about pennies. A Haitian friend Tiffany met at the hospital volunteered to drive Tiffany to Yveline's home, clear across the other side of the city. After a forty-five-minute drive they were in the neighborhood, but they were unsure of the exact house. In an e-mail she sent to me, Tiffany picks up the story:

So I began to tremble again thinking I wasn't going to be able to find her. Some of the homes on her street were destroyed and some were still standing. I finally saw an older woman in the back yard of a home sweeping. The feeling in my stomach told me it was Yveline's grandmother. I jumped out of the car and began yelling, Yveline, Yveline! The women looked up and dropped her broomstick and yelled for Yveline. Yveline began running in one direction and I headed in the opposite. I began laughing because as simple as it sounds I couldn't tell her to stop or go to her right. She doesn't speak English, so I stopped and waited for her to find me! She looked absolutely beautiful—her bright smile and brown eyes shined just like I remembered! The wounds on her face healed nicely; still with scarring but such an improvement. She is able to move her hand and wiggle her fingers (which was the first thing she proudly showed me). I smiled and tears welled in my eyes as she looked so deeply into my eyes then hugged me with the strongest hug I've felt! We sat and touched each other's hands and smiled. I asked her if she'd like to come and play with me for the day via an interpreter. I took her answer as a yes as she ran quickly into her room, changed her clothes into something nicer, and ran back out pulling my hand to leave! I promised her grandmother that I would have her home by 7 p.m. that night and that I would take great care of her! We sat in the car and stared at each other and began laughing. She instantly began teaching me Creole. She would say words in English then Creole and have me repeat them. I would do the same back! I was shocked that her English had improved so much— still not to the point of being able to have a full conversation, but close!! The feeling in my heart is something that only she can create! It's so hard to describe because I only feel it when I'm with her, she has brightened my heart in so many ways. I can truly see the Lord in her and working through her—yet she is so young. She loves to laugh and play like any ordinary child, she loves to color, paint, play with dolls, and swim. The first day had to come to an end, but thankfully I knew I had another day to spend with her.

The next day we picked her up again, only she knew we were coming and we knew where she lived! She was perched on her steps anticipating our arrival—she ran out to the car and jumped in. We drove back to my friend's house and during the drive I asked her if she was hungry. She answered, "Yes, I couldn't sleep or eat yesterday and today because I was excited to see you again." I smiled and hugged her. During the day we played again in the pool, ate delicious Haitian food, and enjoyed every minute we had. That day was particularly special as Yveline asked if she could call me her "mom." I looked at her and said, "Yveline, you can call me anything you want—you know I love you and you know your mom in heaven loves you too." From that moment forward, even today, she calls me mom! Again, my heart feels wonderful knowing that I can love this child with my whole heart and she knows she can do the same. She and I had an amazing two days together, days I will cherish forever!!

The end of the day had to come to an end as the sun was setting over the mountaintops in Port-au-Prince. She looked at me and asked me to stay with her. She promised I could sleep in her bed and she would sleep next to me . . . we could play together all day she said! I began to cry because so much of me wanted to say yes but reality has it that I had to return to Chicago in the morning. We drove Yveline home and tears filled our eyes the entire ride. I kept telling her I love her and that I will be back soon. I promised her that! She would look at me and shake her head and say, "No, stay with me!" We finally arrived at her home and her grandmother was waiting for her, Yveline reluctantly got out of the car and walked to her grandmother's side . . . that image burns in my heart because that was the exact situation the last time I said goodbye to her in January. I hugged and kissed her forehead and told her to eat every day and sleep every day and one day soon I would be back to pick her up! Her grandmother told her something that confirms that our hearts are forever locked! Remy translated to me that her grandmother told Yveline, "Yveline, your mommy will be back soon. This mommy will be back soon, please don't be sad—she loves you and will be back!" I know I didn't tell her grandmother she calls me mom, so Yveline truly must look to me as her mother! My heart sank in my throat as my commitment to this young girl is forever united and I am so excited! I am so thankful that the Lord spared this child in order for me to meet her. She has and forever will amaze me with her love and grace for everyone. I know the Lord created our bond and because we are both children of Him He will keep our hearts together forever!

On Tuesday I found myself at the hillside site of the totally destroyed major seminary where many seminarians and professors lost their lives. I actually was able to walk inside some of the collapsed building. In the kitchen area I could see large cans of tomato sauce that were being opened in preparation for the evening's meal. It was haunting to see how life was abruptly interrupted . . . and ended. Rats scurried through the clutter of religious articles, books, and clothes. I picked up a book titled *What Is Faith?* . . . a title which took on added poignancy in that dreadful setting.

My birthday fell smack in the middle of Holy Week, on Wednesday, March 31. That morning I left the hotel before 6:00 a.m. and drove to downtown Port-au-Prince. Traffic was light and the trip was quick. The day before I learned from a French photographer that it was possible to climb the interior stairs of a tall monument across from the Presidential Palace. The steel structure towers over downtown, and the top platform offers a spectacular panoramic view of the city. The monument vaguely resembles the Eiffel Tower, but it is far uglier and lacks any sense of grace or style. People were taking refuge on the ground floor of the monument. One naked man, who had his back to me, was in the process of pulling up his shorts. A woman was sleeping on the concrete floor, an infant in her arms. The floor was littered with trash. I slowly climbed the ten or so floors to the top. With each ascending floor, the structure became narrower.

The view was so stunning that I felt like a whirling dervish, circling the platform, feverishly snapping photographs and filming from every direction. It was a slightly overcast morning and the diffused lighting was perfect, as the sun gently broke through the clouds. The unobstructed view of the collapsed Presidential Palace truly excited me. Off in the distance, the morning light was gently dancing on the ocean. And from every direction I could look down and see a sea of tents.

After about twenty minutes of nonstop photographing and filming, I put the cameras down, and for the next thirty minutes I stood silently looking out over the city. As I looked down at the destroyed city of Port-au-Prince, my mind flashed back fifteen years ago, to March 31, 1995, when I stood atop Mount Subasio in Italy and looked down on the ancient city of Assisi. Two weeks earlier, I had my dramatic and totally unexplainable encounter with God in an empty church in Rome that forever altered my life and put me on the road to places of severe poverty in slums of overwhelming need around the world. I tried to meditate on the meaning of it all.

While I was standing there, my film on Saint Francis, *The Loneliness and Longing of St. Francis of Assisi,* was being manufactured back in California. I made the film because after the horror of Uganda I could no longer take seeing any more starving and dying kids. I needed to enter more deeply into the spirituality of Saint Francis. But now I am back in the middle of intense suffering, in the middle of death. Despite some of the good things happening here, Haiti seemed to be pushing me toward a sense of absolute hopelessness. What am I doing? Is any of this—the films, the books, the speaking—making any difference?

My life's story since March of 1995 has been shaped, as best as I am able to allow it and despite my failures, by the gospel story, and it is my hope that my work adds a little something to the reality of

God's all-inclusive love and mercy. Still, I wonder what my story and the poverty-stricken places I've seen mean for me. How can I even begin to fix the poverty I see around me when I do not truly see the poverty within me? The more I see of life, the fewer answers I have. It is all such an unfathomable mystery . . . life, death, love, hatred, joy, sadness, health, sickness, prosperity, poverty, laughter, suffering. Yet God, through Christ, is in all of it, except hatred, of course. It is all part of the magnificent complexity of the mystery of creation.

O God, help me let go of everything in my life and all that I expect and wish for. I know that You have the best plan for me, and I am trying to give You everything: my life, my time, my possessions, and my aspirations. Help me to wait upon You and not take matters into my own hands. I want to give You my all and I believe with all my heart and strength that You will take care of me, far and above anything I could ever do. I love you, Lord, and I want all of my life to be my gift to You. Help me, please, dear Lord, let go of everything that keeps me from being more fully united to You.

Lord, help me grow in humility, help me to confess my own brokenness. Help me move out of my world of illusion and self-created desires and into Your universe of love, joy, and peace.

Lord, I cry out for healing. Transform my brokenness, I beg You, into a new life in You, the true source of strength and wholeness.

Help me, Lord, remove everything that blocks me from joyfully living the good news of the paschal mystery. O awesome and transcendent God, free me from the slavery of my sinfulness.

In my prison of darkness, Your unmerited grace is a soothing ray of light.

After leaving the monument, I drove to Cité Soleil for a visit with Father Tom Hagan. He lives about a fifteen-minute drive away from Cité Soleil, in a poor residential neighborhood that does have some larger homes. Driving down his block I saw that many of the homes had collapsed. When I entered his compound I was initially disoriented. The five-story home, which housed Father Tom and the seminarians, was gone, and all the rubble had been removed. There was only a large open area. After warmly greeting me, Father Tom pointed out the tile floor from the porch area of the house. "We sat right there when we first met," he said. You could clearly see the outline of where the house once stood, bursting with activity and prayer. Now . . . nothing. The open space is now the staging area for the distribution of food.

The back half of the property once was a garden area. It is now covered with tents. Three more substantial, yet clearly temporary, structures give shelter to a small office for Father Tom, a kitchen and dining area, and a storage unit. Four or five seminarians were seated at the table in the kitchen area, each busy reading and writing. Life is going on. At the back of the garden area, two of the seminarians killed in the quake are buried. Their memorial is part of a small, outdoor chapel featuring the few items that were pulled from the rubble of the chapel once located in the main house. Most notable was a large, almost life-sized, carved wooden depiction of the body of Christ on the cross.

Father Tom looked and sounded physically and emotionally exhausted. We sat in the garden chapel and talked for a while, as he shared with me the horror of the moment of the earthquake and his narrow escape from death. He has been living in a tent. He misses his early morning prayer time in the old chapel, his time of "having a cup of coffee with the Lord." Now it's harder to make the coffee, and worse he is surrounded by rats in his new outdoor chapel. And he misses the simple pleasure of his old bathroom; he is not too thrilled with his new primitive "bathroom." Everything now is a struggle. He has virtually no material possessions. He misses the photos of his mother. Yet he does not complain . . . even though he is currently struggling with painful kidney stones. It seemed clear he was just trying to get through Holy Week so he could return to the States for treatment.

It was truly delightful for me to have a chance to sit alone with Father Tom and have a leisurely conversation. Everything he had, his chapel, his way of life, abruptly ended. But he said he was not really sad, he was just trying to adjust to a new chapter in his life, and anticipating what had to be done to rebuild the schools and reestablish all the medical and social services he offered. He thinks of all he did over the years . . . and now he must let it all go. Still, he said, "I crave a little normalcy." But he accepts that he must be satisfied with his daily bread, as he searches to discover what the Lord is teaching him.

He knows now how easy it is to reach the point, that arid place in the spiritual desert, where you must turn to God and say, "God, I really need You now." There is no individual survival in Cité Soleil. "We need God . . . and we need each other," he said, adding, "But the culture says we should know what we are doing all the time, you should be in control, that you should have everything in control, that you should be totally self-sufficient. Well, that's the advice of a fool." He went on to say that we are taught to take care of ourselves first, which is exactly what we want to hear. "But the problem is," he opined, "if you take care of yourself first you will die spiritually and humanly. We are three dimensional . . . we need to love ourselves, others, and God all at the same time, which creates a synergy of love. Without any of those three dimensions, we become less human, less alive. All the evils of the world, I think, have been caused by one-dimensional people, people just focused on themselves. The culture is forcing us to be one-dimensional people."

He paused for a moment, looking off into the trees. Then he said, "If we are in a certain place and the other is suffering, we have to suffer with them. And that is what is happening here. So, I don't know where we are going, but I would say that I am more confident that the people here in Haiti will survive. They in many ways are much more human and alive than many of the people in the States, some of whom are on the verge of losing their humanity and also their own authenticity, who they were born to be. People are trying to fill expectations they can't fulfill. The price they pay is they are becoming less alive, less human. Down here people still smile, still enjoy a sunset and little jokes. But I can't indict anyone or any culture. I can't speak with authority about anything."

That last sentence was pure Father Tom. After being prompted to speak with sparkling insight, he immediately retreats into a position of sincere humility. He hates being interviewed.

He lamented how the more you help the poor of Cité Soleil, the more they want. He struggles to deal with the dishonesty and anger that often surfaces when people are in the survival mode. At one point I asked him about Salesian spirituality. He said Saint Francis de Sales was very human, and he believed everyone was called to be holy. According to the saint, everyone needed to have confidence in God. But if you don't have confidence, tell God you don't have confidence, because it is really His problem. The priest added, almost with a chuckle, "Sometimes I am ready to say to the Lord I'm losing confidence in You too . . . where the heck have You been?" But his point was more profound. He said, "You just know that the same loving God who took care of you yesterday will take care of you today and will take care of you tomorrow. So what you really have is what I call a positive arrogance. You wake up and know nothing will bother you. The spirituality of Saint Francis de Sales is really about taking every moment as it comes. But you can't do that without prayer, without the discipline of being still and beginning the day alone with the Lord."

Like the founder of his religious order, Father Tom is also very human and a man of deep faith who truly does take every moment as it comes.

After our talk, we drove to Cité Soleil. Father Tom wanted to check in with a team of volunteer structural engineers from Southern California who were evaluating each of his schools. The engineers' trip was arranged through Holy Family Church in South Pasadena. Temporary classrooms were being constructed in the open spaces on the campuses of some of the schools, and classes had already partially resumed. The dedication and drive of Father Tom and the Hands Together staff is truly remarkable. They are distributing food and water, rebuilding the schools, and simply being a beautiful presence of Christ's love and mercy.

Father Tom graciously invited me to attend and film the Holy Thursday, Good Friday, and Easter Sunday services in Cité Soleil . . . even though he is not fond of cameras or publicity.

When I arrived at Father Tom's compound on Holy Thursday, he seemed a bit down. He told me that some gang members from Cité Soleil had threatened to kill two of his top staff people, both Haitians and reformed gang members, as well as the security guard at the compound. It is all impossible to fathom. Living with the destruction and profound need is hard enough, but adding the element of vengeful violence intensifies the situation to the breaking point. No wonder Father Tom is so fed up with everything. Yet, he still has this gentle calmness about him . . . softly walking through an endless valley of death, fearing nothing, his eyes fixed on God. It took Father Tom two days to defuse the threat of violence.

Hundreds of people attended the Holy Thursday liturgy. For me the most impactful moment was when Father Tom washed the feet of the poor. I had anticipated that a few people would come up near the altar and he would wash their feet as representatives of the gathered community. But no, that is not what happened. The liturgy was held in an outdoor space that was extremely narrow and rectangular in shape. There was room for only four rows of seats, extremely long rows. The altar was placed in front of the outer wall of the school. When it came time for the foot washing, Father Tom got down on his knees and crawled along the concrete floor from person to person seated in the long, front row, removing their shoes and lovingly washing and drying their feet. Most of the people in the front row were old. It was inspiring to watch Father Tom struggling to move from person to person, clearly in some degree of discomfort from the heat, the hard ground, and the sheer physical exertion. He washed at least fifty pairs of feet.

After the liturgy, Father Tom threw me a curve ball. I had not anticipated that he was going to process through the streets of Cité Soleil with the Blessed Sacrament. As he left the walled school property, followed by a procession of virtually all the participants at the liturgy, including at least one old man with an amputated leg, Father Tom walked around the block on which the school is located. It was a large block, and the walk took at least fifteen minutes. As we passed the shacks that lined the road, many of the people offered a sign of reverence. At one point, armed United Nations soldiers briefly trailed us. I walked the entire circumference of the block backwards, filming and photographing Father Tom as he led the procession.

When we returned to the compound, Hands Together distributed a large bag of rice to all in attendance.

Saint Francis of Assisi understood we all are the human face of Jesus; he knew that all of humanity makes up the divine face. God assumed flesh and was born into a world of oppression and persecution. Can we ever grasp the reality of the divine presence dwelling in a depraved humanity and that consequently every man, woman, and child is uniquely precious, equal, and blessed, all brothers and sisters? Jesus is hungry and naked. Yet we build and decorate elaborate churches in His name, but do not feed or clothe Him. Every day,

God comes to us in a distressing disguise, clothed in the rags of a tormented and neglected poor person, in hopes that the encounter will provide a place for healing and hurt to meet, for grace to embrace sin, for beauty to be restored.

As Father Daniel O'Leary writes: "It takes a great love, and many deaths, to transform the eyes of our souls so as to see God's face in every face. And inevitably, inexorably, this love, this hope, will lead to a crucifixion."

One of the more poignant moments of my time with Father Tom came when he invited me into his little shoe box of a temporary office, just barely large enough to fit a desk for his computer, a chair, and a few cabinets. On one wall hung a crucifix that instantly caught my attention, because, even at first glance, it seemed to contain the story of the earthquake in all its agony and spiritual depth. The crucifix once hung in the bedroom of Father Tom's parents. It was fairly large, perhaps about two feet tall. The cross was made of wood that had been painted black. The corpus of Christ was white, made,

I think, of plaster. After the death of his parents, Father Tom has always had the crucifix with him, no matter his assignment. In Haiti, the crucifix hung in the chapel inside his home.

The crucifix was also hidden in the rubble. And when it was pulled out, Christ was missing his arms and legs. All that remained were thin strands of metal to which once clung the figure's extremities. In a country where so many people lost arms and legs, so did the figure of Christ. It was as if Christ had once again given himself fully, suffered right alongside his flock. Christ was one with the Haitians also hidden in the rubble. He had allowed himself to once again be wounded and disfigured. Christ without arms and legs is still hanging from the wooden cross, still with us, still feeling our pain and agony, still pointing to the love and mercy of God. I took many photographs of the wounded crucifix, because for me, that one graphic image perfectly symbolized the tragedy that had befallen the nation of Haiti. And Christ was there, hidden in the suffering, hidden in the death.

On Good Friday I once again returned to Father Tom's compound, and we drove to Cité Soleil. After a brief prayer service, Father

Tom, with the help of a few seminarians, hoisted the large wooden cross on his shoulders and began a long march through Cité Soleil, followed by a procession of people singing and praying. It was at least a twenty-minute walk from the school to the wharf, where we turned around and walked back. As we approached the school, he turned right and once more circled the large block on which the school rests. Somewhere along the way, one of the seminarians relieved Father Tom from the heavy burden of carrying the cross. It was a truly inspiring walk past the endless shacks that lined the main street.

Once back within the borders of the school, Father Tom led all in more prayers and the service ended with each person venerating and kissing the cross.

Saint Rafael Arnáiz Barón, the Spanish Trappist Oblate brother who died in 1938, said, "God is in the Cross, and as long as we do not love the Cross, we will not see him, or feel him. . . . If the world and men knew. . . . But they will not know; they are very busy in their interests; their hearts are very full of things that are not God." Statements such as that are hard to hear. Such fervor for the Cross seems extreme. Yet somehow, I fear it is true. I know I want to avoid the Cross. I know my heart is full of things not of God.

O sweet Lord I want so very much to avoid the bitter cross You ask me to carry, the cross of putting aside everything that is outside the realm of Your love. Actually, nothing is outside the realm of Your love, because You so long for us, so thirst for us, that You follow us into the darkest corners of our lives looking to embrace us with Your mercy and compassion. Yet I so often want to embrace things that You find unhealthy and unfitting for a seeker of God.

O Lord help me see, feel, and know that outside of You there is nothing of any worth, and that with You all is priceless. Help me nail to the cross the secret things in my heart that I must sacrifice in order to follow You more closely and love You more dearly.

In the abandonment, despair, and conflict of Holy Saturday I drove to Léogâne, which was the epicenter of the quake, about ninety minutes west of Port-au-Prince. The level of devastation was frightening. Very little of the town remained standing. Yet amid the massive amounts of rubble, people were busy clearing the debris. At one location, the destroyed home of the parish priest, at least seventy-five people had gathered together under the blazingly hot sun to undertake the painstakingly hard, back-breaking job of breaking up the large pieces of concrete and then hauling them away in buckets and wheel barrels. The young and old, men and women, and kids all pitched in. A number of teenage boys wore Boy Scout uniforms. Everyone was working together, doing what had to be done, in order to start over. Many of the mountains of rubble were tombs. And on Holy Saturday we remember Christ's time in the tomb. In the Paschal Mystery, suffering and hope are intertwined. The suffering of Good Friday was a portal to the hope of Easter Sunday.

For me, there was no better place to celebrate Easter than in Cité Soleil with Father Tom Hagan. As I drove across Port-au-Prince to Cité Soleil, I was impressed by the number of people on their way to church services, all decked out in their finest clothes. It was a joy to see so many beautiful young girls dressed in pretty white dresses and handsome young boys in neatly pressed suits, dress shirts, and ties. They were all walking past mountains of rubble, yet dressed like royalty on the way to meet their king.

Father Tom's main celebration of Easter began at 9:00 a.m. along the outer wall of one of his schools in the heart of Cité Soleil. It was a joyful celebration accompanied by drums and lots of singing and waving hands. The faces of the Haitians, both old and young, seemed to sparkle with more radiant beauty than usual. Immediately after the Mass we drove less than a mile to an area of Cité Soleil known as Port Jeremiah. Father Tom said it was the worst part of the slum . . . something I found hard to even imagine. The liturgy was held under a large sheet to shield us from the sun. Before it began, Father Tom was in such severe pain from his kidney stones, he needed some morphine just to get through the service. There were many kids and some Italian missionary sisters present. It too was a joyful celebration, as the Alleluias drifted over the garbage-strewn landscape and rusted metal shacks.

As Father Daniel O'Leary reminds us: "The whole Passover

experience is for the grounding and anchoring of us during the pain and passion of our lives, for our coming home to the wonder and challenge of our true identity in God. This is our hidden self revealed." Purified and emptied by Lent, Easter is a time to embrace the divinity within us, time for us to shine with the radiance of the Risen Lord and to share our invisible beauty with all of creation through the tenderness of our words and touch.

I am so happy and thankful that I followed my heart to Haiti before the earthquake. Had I not, I would have watched those tragic events of January 12 unfold before me on television, glued to the coverage for a few days . . . and then, sadly, I would have moved on to matters of more pressing concern to me personally. But once I had, by God's grace, walked among the people of Haiti, mingled with them, saw their dreadful plight and had an encounter with that reluctant and unlikely saint, Father Tom Hagan, I had no other option but to return to Haiti at least twice after the earthquake. Haiti is now embedded in my soul, stamped on my psyche. Life after Haiti, for me, will be filtered through the lens of Haiti. I know I will return. Life is so very, very real and basic here. And as my third trip to Haiti ended, I humbly offered this simple prayer:

O God, help me follow wherever You lead me. I believe my spiritual life is essentially a journey in which I move from what I am to what I will become. I am just beginning to learn that life is a journey to weakness. The saints truly learned to live when they began to explore their own weaknesses. By Your unmerited grace, every experience of weakness is an opportunity of growth and renewed life. Weaknesses transformed by the reality of Christ's love become life-giving virtues.

The emptiness I often feel stems from not realizing I am made for communion with You. If I am not growing toward unity with You, my God, I am then growing apart from You. Help me learn to be still, to be humble in order to move into a greater union with You. Only in stillness and humility can I enter into a dialogue with You, sweet Jesus. I need to bring to You what I am so that in time I might become more like what You are.

In following you, Lord Jesus, I have seen with my own eyes in so many places around the world how life is filled to overflowing with pain and struggle. Your way leads to the Cross, and it doesn't offer an easy way around it. To become Your disciple means accepting a spirituality of the cross and renouncing a spirituality of glory. You humbled yourself in order to love me. You gave of yourself in order to love me. Help me give myself in order to love You and all of creation.

And the day after I left, the rains came, pouring more misery on the poor people of Haiti, people whose beautiful spirit of resilience will once more be put to the test. I have no doubt they will triumph. I know I wouldn't.

The Portal of Mysticism

At least twice in these pages I have struggled to come to grips with suffering, and God's role in it. In our postmodern world, the massive global suffering is an overwhelming issue that we do not discuss, in part, I suppose, because we do not know what to say. If God exists and for whatever reason does not elect to respond in some tangible way to the anguish so many endure, then what is the point of caring about God or pondering God's apparent inaccessibility? It seems to me that the struggle for social justice is an immense part in our relationship to Christ that sparks our imagination and helps us enter more productively into the silence of God. In our evolving relationship with God we eventually reach a point where all words fail, and it is at this point we enter the portal of mysticism, which is our only saving hope. In this realm, silence precedes (and often supersedes) speech, and here art is more important than logic. It is here that we begin living a more spiritual (and less religious) life. The emphasis on doctrine and dogma decreases as the emphasis on love and service increases. When it comes to suffering, we need to ask questions, but the answers will be found only in silence and stillness, which must lead us to do whatever we can to lessen the suffering.

For me, the anguish of Haiti pushes me deeper into prayer, deeper into the heart of God. Being in a situation of extreme suffering makes it easy to strip away all that is inessential or superficial. In Haiti my prayer life became more vibrant and real. And I could see, however opaquely, God hidden in the rubble.

Perhaps this entry is a prime example of the futility of words when discussing the mystery of God. Perhaps I should delete it.

Lifeless and Homeless

The terrible suffering of the people in Haiti is a result of the centuries of human inhumanity to other humans that cumulatively resulted in Haiti ending up with no infrastructure, no support system, nothing to help them when the earth shook their homes down on them, killing more than 300,000 people and leaving more than a million people homeless. The monumental size and scope of the devastation leaves us speechless and disoriented.

When, in the face of such destruction, we ask, "Where is God?," we are in essence screaming into the darkness, "Why?" Why has the life been so painfully snuffed out of so many? Why are so many enduring the excruciating pain of severe crush injuries? Why are so many kids instantly orphans?

Some, in their utter disbelief in what they are seeing, blame God. Or, in the case of one misguided, insensitive, and spiritually ignorant televangelist, blame the Haitians, claiming that centuries ago they made a pact with the devil.

The truth is that neither God nor the devil nor innocent dead or homeless Haitians had anything to do with the incomprehensible suffering that followed the earthquake. In our grief-stricken hearts, we cannot comprehend so much death, so much pain, so much sadness, and so we are shocked out of our innocence and into the stark-naked reality that humanity is vulnerable. Humanity is vulnerable to the greed and abuse of power exercised over the centuries by those who have banished a loving and merciful God from the equation of their lives, leaving them free to rape and pillage innocent souls and fertile land. These godless, power-hungry men (including men from the United States government and commerce) have stripped countless peasants of their God-given dignity and left them absolutely powerless and imprisoned in a modern form of slavery, unable to even feed themselves. Sadly, during much of Haiti's history, some of it rather recent, the church turned its back on the poor and sided with the rich and powerful elite. And when and where the church does not side with the poor and powerless, it is no longer the church of Jesus . . . it is nothing more than a social club for people pretending to be religious.

If we love God, we should try to emulate God's behavior, but we, for the most part, don't. God gathers. We scatter. God unites. We divide. God embraces. We exclude. And so we get Haiti. It really is that simple.

The Larger Calamity

On that dreadful Tuesday afternoon in January, Port-au-Prince was, in a blink of an eye, pushed off a cliff into an abyss of despair. How should a follower of Christ respond to such a catastrophe? Or, on a bigger picture, how should a follower of Christ respond to the systemic evils of racism, hatred, injustice, poverty, and the countless deaths from preventable diseases? In response to the news reports from Haiti, churches all across the United States and around the world responded with great generosity by writing checks to reputable relief organizations, which was vitally important to Haiti's recovery. But the larger calamity is the silent hunger, sickness, and death that march on without notice year after year destroying countless lives in many developing nations. This larger calamity has yet to penetrate the consciousness of most Christians. Sure, we are vaguely aware of the plight of the chronically poor around the world, but we do not see a steady stream of heart-breaking images that can rally the world, at least for a short period of time, to action the way they did after natural disasters such as the hurricane-induced flooding in New Orleans, the tsunami in Indonesia, and the earthquake in Haiti.

My job (actually my vocation) is to capture and show images from the silent, unseen disasters that are happening every day all around the world and in our own backyard in cities such as Philadelphia, Detroit, and Los Angeles, where I have spent many brutally sad and dispiriting months with the homeless, including thousands upon thousands of innocent children living in cars, tents, and overcrowded missions, surrounded by drugs, mental illness, and violence. But it is not only despair that I capture with my camera, for if it were, I would simply put a gun to my head now to escape the chamber of torture that I have witnessed. What I also capture is hope, hope writ large by the lives of quiet, everyday, humble saints, who truly exemplify the self-emptying love of Christ and who are a manifestation of God's boundless love and mercy in the lives of the neglected poor who have known nothing but misery. I want to end this section of the book with a brief visit to a place that broke my heart long before Haiti and still haunts me . . . a place you need to know about and help.

Cathedrals of the Poor

In 2008, I made three trips to Uganda. The nearly two months I spent in that war-torn nation in East Africa had profound impact on me.

In sub-Saharan East Africa, amid lush landscapes, offering an almost Eden-like existence, is one of the saddest places on Earth. Once part of a prosperous ancient African kingdom, Uganda is now struggling back onto its feet after half a century of unimaginable pain and suffering. Half of Uganda's thirty-one million people do not have access to clean, safe water, making them vulnerable to cholera and diarrhea. Respiratory illnesses are widespread. Less than 10 percent of the population has access to electricity. About 90 percent of Uganda's total energy requirements are met using firewood and charcoal. About 80 percent of the population lives in villages and small trading centers.

Most women do not live beyond their early 50s; men live even shorter lives. The infant mortality rate and life expectancy are among the worst in the world. Children are a vital part of the household economy, and their families need them to work in the home or fields. Only half the boys and about 25 percent of the girls complete primary school. Only about 15 percent finish secondary school. About 65 percent of the adults are illiterate. Sixty-five percent of Ugandans live below the poverty line, on less than the equivalent of $15 a month.

The northern part of Uganda has been ravaged by a brutal civil war for more than twenty years. The people, mostly peaceful, rural farmers, lived in constant fear of rebel attacks, which were launched daily and nightly from the Sudanese border. Few people in the West are aware of the horrifying wave of violence triggered by a rebellious guerrilla group known as the L.R.A.—the Lord's Resistance Army. The L.R.A.'s tactics were beyond despicable. One of their primary tools was the routine kidnapping of children. The L.R.A. kidnapped children as young as seven years old and trained them to fight and kill in their army. While the captured boys were turned into killing machines, the captured young girls became sex slaves and are given to rebel commanders as trophies for military victories. For every ten girls who were lucky enough to escape from the L.R.A., nine had been infected with AIDS. An estimated 40,000 children were abducted, tortured, and forced to become child soldiers or "wives" in the L.R.A.

The war has killed, maimed, raped, and displaced well over a million people. In order to survive, this displaced population was forced to live in IDP (internally displaced persons) camps. The displacement camps in Gulu and Lira were nothing short of a nightmare. Until very recently, some camps had as many as 60,000 people crammed into a small space, living in squalor and with an array of deadly diseases. They lived without electricity and access to clean water. Health care was virtually nonexistent. The morbidity rates in the fetid camps were horrifying; at its worst point, it was estimated that 1,000 people were dying each week. Girls and young women living in the camps routinely suffered sexual and physical abuse.

Memories of my time in the camps, seeing so many naked, starving kids with bloated bellies, still haunts me. Shortly after we completed the film, a cease-fire was negotiated and has, with the exception of a few eruptions of violence, held now for nearly two years. Mercifully, the IDP camps have slowly emptied.

I did not think it was possible to find a more desperate nation than Uganda. Yet, Haiti seemed worse to me . . . even before the earthquake. After the earthquake, there is no question that Haiti is the most desperate place on earth. The film I made about Uganda is titled *The Fragrant Spirit of Life*. Near the end of part 2 of the four-hour-long film, there is a short meditation titled "The Cathedrals of the Poor," in which I expressed why places such as Uganda were important to my spiritual growth. Here is a portion of the text of the narration from the film.

This is the kind of place where I come when I really want to com-mune with God, a place where ramshackle huts are stained-glass windows of heaven through which the light of God pours.

For me, the far-too-numerous and massive slums that dot the landscape of so many developing nations are Cathedrals of the Poor, places so real and raw that they pulsate with the presence of God. In these slums, you are on holy ground because Jesus is here in the form of people suffering from hunger and curable dis-eases.

Christ wants us to live a life of detachment and expectation. But we cling to the countless things we think are important. We chase after what we don't have; we lust after what is beyond our reach. We have turned greed and hoarding into virtues. Consumed by our need for comfort and security, we have become blinded to the needs of the poor. We do not share, and our selfishness is the cause of much of the poverty we see.

Economic policies in affluent nations often have a devastating impact on destitute people living in destitute countries, making basic human dignity something that is far beyond their reach.

The people in the massive slums of Kampala have no voice, no power, no rights . . . and no way to make their plight known.

Uganda, for me, it turned out, was a preparation for what I saw and felt in Haiti. How is it that we continue to turn a blind eye toward the stupendous amounts of human suffering and agony that blankets so much of the world?

The Cross and Suffering

Haiti and Uganda make it abundantly clear that poverty is painful. But far beneath the surface, you find the priceless seed of hope. Not just a fairy-tale hope, but a gritty hope rooted in total dependency on God. As I walked with the poor, I encountered my own true poverty and the radical truth of the gospel: only empty hands can hold God. My encounter with the bloated belly of poverty revealed the radical nature of Christianity.

Jesus showed us how to love, how to love unconditionally and without limits. And according to Christ, how we love the hungry, the lowly, and the lost is how we love him; and how we love Christ will be the only litmus test for our entrance into our heavenly home with God for all eternity. And until we enter our eternal home, we are all homeless, even if we live in a palace, because everything on earth is perishable . . . except love.

We are all brothers and sisters, children of the same Creator, and to set ourselves up as higher or better than others is a subtle form of blasphemy. We are all connected, one with all of creation and the Creator. If one among us is diminished, we are all diminished.

The Incarnation teaches us that God is humble. The richness of God is revealed in the poverty of Christ. God lives in our poverty and weakness. Jesus embraced and loved the poor and rejected. For Jesus, the poor are sacraments, because they offer a direct way to encounter God. The poor, broken, and rejected are portals through which we can enter fully into the life of Christ.

Christ shows us that mercy is more than compassion or justice. Mercy requires us to become one with the poor and hurting, to live their misery as though it were our own. In Christ, we see a God so generous he gives himself away out of love. Christ moved beyond justice to generosity.

My exposure to those saddled with extreme poverty uncovered my own clinging selfishness. I came to see how consuming more than I needed was stealing from those in need.

Perhaps Saint Francis understood that it would be hard for him to feel true compassion for the poor and the weak as long he sought comfort and required security for himself. I think Saint Francis of Assisi understood that compassion was far removed from pity and sympathy . . . that compassion grew out of an awareness of our common humanity. For Saint Francis service to the poor was not optional . . . it was a requirement for the follower of Christ.

While we busy ourselves striving for power and control, the gospel proclaims a far different approach: live a life of utter dependence on and receptivity to God. By accepting that gospel approach, spiritual growth and fulfillment become possible. The gospel invites us to live with contradiction—when one has nothing, one has everything.

When we hear the cries of the oppressed, the cries of the poor, we hear the voice of God. Where there is weakness, there is God. We need to ask God to shatter our complacency, to strip us of our need for comfort.

If the gospel is not about love and justice, it has been reduced to mere sentimentality. Jesus denounced power that leads to injustice and poverty. He asked us to share what we have with others. Christianity does not turn away from the cross and suffering; it enters it. Of course, we don't like hearing that.

In *New Seeds of Contemplation,* Thomas Merton wrote: "The ultimate perfection of the contemplative life is not a heaven of separate individuals, each one viewing his own private intuition of God; it is a sea of Love which flows through the One Body of all the elect, all the angels and saints, and their contemplation would be incomplete if it were not shared, or if it were shared with fewer souls, or with spirits capable of less vision and less joy."

One More Piece of Love and Goodness

In the face of such massive destruction and monstrous loss of life, it is easy to lose faith, to begin to doubt and even to succumb to hopelessness. Walking around Port-au-Prince after the earthquake one could easily think that God was absent. As we approached Holy Week I was graced with the opportunity to dip once more into the writings of Etty Hillesum, a Jewish mystic who was incarcerated and killed in a concentration camp. In the dreadful darkness of Westerbork camp, her final days were marked by her shining compassion, which she extended even to the Germans who were committing heinous atrocities. She insisted her fellow prisoners love their enemies, because deep down no one is really bad. She wrote, "Every atom of hate added to the world makes it an even more inhospitable place." She said that Jesus' advice not to worry about tomorrow was the only way to survive the camps. She wrote, "The misery here is really indescribable. People live in those big barracks like so many rats in a sewer. There are many children dying." Yet, she never doubted for a second God's presence, even in the midst of the deprivation, filth, and suffering of the camp. In such a place of extreme horror and evil, Etty was able to write: "Those two months behind barbed wire have been the richest two months of my life, in which my highest values were so deeply confirmed. . . . I am so grateful to You God, for having made my life so rich." Etty Hillesum died in Auschwitz on November 30, 1943, at the age of twenty-nine.

I want to begin to draw this book to a close with a quote from a letter dated July 3, 1943, that Etty wrote to her family:

The misery here is quite terrible; and yet, at night when the day has slunk way into the depths behind me, I often walk with a spring in my step along the barbed wire. And then time and again, it soars straight from my heart, . . . the feeling that life is glorious and magnificent, and that one day we shall build a whole new world. Against every new outrage and every fresh horror, we shall put up one more piece of love and goodness.

Those exact words could have been written in a letter by a young woman from Haiti living in a refugee camp, having lost many family and friends. And I think those poignant words underscore the only way that Haiti will recover, rebuild, and renew itself . . . that is, with love and goodness, and huge amounts of both for a long period of time. It really is time we rebuild our lives, our communities, and our world on the eternal principles that cannot be destroyed by Nazis, brutal dictators, gangs, terrorists, or earthquakes. We need to see God in each other. We need to turn away from hatred and more fully embrace love. We need to make compassion the foundation of our lives and actions. Tolstoy said that our great duty as humans was to sow the seed of compassion in each other's hearts. And it is only compassion that will change and save the world. And Anne Frank reminds us, "How wonderful it is that nobody need wait a single moment before starting to improve the world."

Epilogue
A Beggar of Love

In my book *Thoughts of a Blind Beggar*, I wrote that we are all blind beggars who need to hold outstretched, empty hands to God, who will give us a new vision and all that we need.

Well, I think the truth is actually more fundamental, more profound than that . . . the truth is that God is also a beggar. God's powerful love for each of us is so great, so far beyond measurement that we, in our blindness, cannot begin to understand it. Yet when it comes to our loving God, God is powerless.

Not only does God not push us, God even tolerates our indifference, our apathy, our detours, our revolts, our faults, failures, and sins. God's love includes the extravagant freedom to accept it or reject it. God desires our love. Yet, God does not interfere, manipulate, or coerce us into loving.

God is a beggar of love, patiently waiting at the door of our soul.

With God, our isolated existence dies and we are born again into a great union of love. Here we can freely enter into a nurturing, life-giving relationship with all of creation, especially with the stranger, the rejected, the isolated, the tormented, and the marginalized, out of which arises a new earth and a new heaven, where prisons of poverty such as Cité Soleil no longer exist.

This pilgrimage to compassion began during Advent, which was truly appropriate. Advent helps us look to the future with hope. But we cannot hope for a better future and remain indifferent to the suffering that currently surrounds us; otherwise, Christian hope is little more than pious escapism. We must act. Human goodness aided by divine help can overcome the dark forces that are holding so many people in a lethal bondage of poverty.

In the light of the miracle of Christmas, we must become, as my Irish friend Father Daniel O'Leary, who lives and works in England, writes: "candles of hope, shining incarnate light on a world and a church lost often in the dark."

Go, be a candle of hope, be a witness and manifestation of God's love by ending hunger and creating peace.

Because of the Incarnation, everything is now graced. Every breath we take matters. Every life matters . . . because every life contains divine potential. God is aware of every tear, every heartache, every physical and emotional wound. God, a beggar of love, is waiting to transform our lives.

I would like to end this Haitian pilgrimage to compassion and the Resurrection with a personal prayer.

Oh God, I have not yet
truly begun to paint
the canvas of my soul.
Help me find the vivid brushstrokes of
love, tenderness, compassion,
wonder, poetry, and purity
needed to create a portrait
inspired by You
to be given as a gift
to all who see it.
Help me replace
the dark, hidden tones
of my life
with the numinous hues
that reveal harmony and balance.
Have the borders
of my canvas
not be so small
as to exclude
the richness and diversity
of all humanity
and the endless paths
to the divine.

For Your Charitable Consideration

Haiti will need serious and committed help for many, many years to come. The following charitable organizations are committed to standing with the Haitian people during the long haul of recovery and rebuilding. Each of them can use your generous support.

Hands Together (Father Tom Hagan): www.handstogether.org
Catholic Relief Services: www.CRS.org
CURE International: www.helpcurenow.org
Partners in Health (Dr. Paul Farmer): www.standwithhaiti.org
Doctors Without Borders: www.doctorswithoutborders.org
Wyoming Haiti Relief (Jill Wanamaker): www.wyominghaitirelief.org